CONFUSION OF TONGUES

CONFUSION OF TONGUES
A Return to Sándor Ferenczi

Miguel Gutiérrez-Peláez

Routledge
Taylor & Francis Group

LONDON AND NEW YORK

Originally published in Argentina in 2012 as *Confusión de lenguas. Un retorno a Sandor Ferenczi* by EUDEM (Editorial de la Universidad de Mar del Plata, Argentina). All rights retained.

First published in English in 2018
by Routledge
2 Park Square, Milton Park, Abingdon, Oxon OX14 4RN

and by Routledge
711 Third Avenue, New York, NY 10017

Routledge is an imprint of the Taylor & Francis Group, an informa business

Copyright © 2018 by Miguel Gutiérrez-Peláez

Translated into English by María Squirru.

British Library Cataloguing-in-Publication Data
A catalogue record for this book is available from the British Library

Library of Congress Cataloging-in-Publication Data
A catalog record has been requested for this book

ISBN: 978-1-78220-572-2 (pbk)

Typeset in Palatino LT Std
by Medlar Publishing Solutions Pvt Ltd, India

To
Verónica, Rodrigo, and Rafael

To
My father

"My dear Karinthy ... You said that you knew two types of wise man and two types of science. The first [type of science] searches for the truth and strives to awaken a sleepy humanity; the second one avoids by all means disturbing the quietude of the drowsy world and even tends to make it fall into a deeper slumber. Psychoanalysis, you said, possesses that special ability to awaken us, trying to give the human psyche, by means of knowledge, not only command over oneself but also of our organic and physical strengths.

But now you write that it is necessary to stop being in [psycho]analysis in order to preferably study those who speak of peace, harmony, welfare, and that, with the help of clever suggestions, including hypnotic dreams, surreptitiously introduce in the human psyche sensations, ideas and reasonable, intelligent, comforting and joyful intentions.

I have previously found your words regarding the power of the wise somewhat audacious, but since then I have been able to convince myself of their certainty. I recognised in principle the ability of "awakener" which corresponded to psychoanalysis and I have not changed my mind, because I am convinced that without an authentic and brave science, any effort to find happiness is useless and at best can only arouse a temporary illusion. But you, on the contrary, have apparently lost patience (possibly due to present miseries); you neither wish the truth nor science and only aspire to find a bit of joy for our tormented world at any price, even if it means lulling it to sleep. In a word, I would simply wish to acknowledge here that, of us two, I am now the one who has not abandoned the ranks of those who awaken."

"Science that lulls and science that awakens."

—A letter to Frigyes Karinthy (Ferenczi, 1924b)

CONTENTS

ACKNOWLEDGEMENTS

This book corresponds for the most part, except for some changes and modifications, to my doctorate in psychology thesis of the Universidad de Buenos Aires, defended in October, 2010. Other writings related to this investigation about Ferenczi have been published in the *Revista Universitaria de Psicoanálisis* (2007, 2008a), *Ideas y Valores* (2008b), *Revista Psicoanálisis* (2008c), the *International Journal of Psychoanalysis* (2009), *Revista Universitas Psychologica* (2010), *Contemporary Psychoanalysis* (2015), *Revista Colombiana de Psiquiatría* (2017a), *Avances en Psicología Latinoamericana* (2017b), *Peace and Conflict: Journal of Peace Psychology* (2017c), amongst others. My masters' thesis in psychoanalysis of the Universidad de Buenos Aires (2006), entitled "Splitting como concepto en la obra de Sándor Ferenczi (Splitting as a concept in Sándor Ferenczi's work)", precedes this book.

I would like to acknowledge those persons who have made the original version of this book, published in Spanish in 2011, possible. Josefina Dartiguelongue, for her tireless friendship, help, and essential contributions; Mauricio Santín, for his affection and for having accompanied me throughout the journey here undertaken; Juan V. Gallardo, for his Ferenczian passion and his invaluable help; Héctor López, whose rigorous supervision and enthusiasm made this book possible;

Marcela Rojas, for her help with the translation of key passages; Horacio Martínez and his team at the Universidad de Mar del Plata for believing in this book and supporting its publication; my teachers, for teaching me and enabling me to stand on my own; my colleagues, for their discussions and energy; my patients, essential for this work and who shall remain anonymous; my parents and Pablo for their unconditional support, and Verónica, my life companion.

Regarding the English version of the book, I would like to thank: Oliver Rathbone, Rachel Rathbone, Constance Govindin, Kate Pearce, and Rod Tweedy from Karnac; Andrea Di Pace and María Ana Barros from EUDEM; Gustavo Quintero, dean of the School of Medicine and Health Sciences at Universidad del Rosario for granting me time and support to work on this project; Juan Felipe Córdoba, editorial director at the Universidad del Rosario, for his help in Frankfurt; Maria Andrea Contreras Nieto and Estefanía Herrán from the Centro de Gestión del Conocimiento y la Innovación (CGCI) of the Universidad del Rosario for their kindness and most diligent work; Stephanie Lavaux, Vicerector of the Universidad del Rosario, and the members of JANUS, for creating a fertile environment to work on this complex topics; Paul Finnegan, for giving the first impulse for the translation of the book into English and establishing the first contact with Karnac; María Squirru, for her great work in the translation of the book; Judit Mészáros, for her kindness during a most fascinating and moving visit to the Ferenczi House in Budapest, as well as for her pertinent comments to the final version of the book; Elías, for his generosity and friendship for permanently granting me valuable contributions to my work; Bernardo and Liliana, for having created in Ubaté a perfect place to work on the English manuscript of the book; to the members and associates of the Nueva Escuela Lacaniana de Bogotá; Miguel Uribe, for his thorough feedback in various of my research products; Emilio Herrera, for his enthusiasm and trust; and Alberto Fergusson, director of the centre for psychosocial studies (CEPSO-CEPSS) of the Universidad del Rosario, and the full members of the centre, for their stimulating ideas in this most fruitful think-tank.

ABOUT THE AUTHOR

Miguel Gutiérrez-Peláez, PhD, is director of the psychology programme of the School of Medicine and Social Sciences at the Universidad del Rosario in Bogotá, Colombia. He directs the scientific psychology journal *Avances en Psicología Latinoamericana* and is a founding member of the Centre for Psychosocial Studies (CEPSO-CEPSS). He is also a member of the interdisciplinary study group on peace and conflict (JANUS) at the Universidad del Rosario. Dr Gutiérrez-Peláez is a psychologist from the Pontificia Universidad Javeriana (PUJ), and has a master's in psychoanalysis and a PhD in psychology from the Universidad de Buenos Aires (UBA). He is a psychoanalyst member of the World Association of Psychoanalysis (AMP) and the Nueva Escuela Lacaniana (NEL). He is also secretary for Colombia of the World Association of Psychosocial Rehabilitation (WAPR). He has taught at different universities in Colombia and Argentina and worked as a clinician in different mental health institutions in Colombia and Argentina. He has worked with Colombian soldiers and police officers who have fought in war zones, as well as with others who have psychological difficulties as a result of involvement in Colombia's armed conflict. Many of his articles dealing with trauma, art, and mental illness, and with psychosocial interventions in armed conflict scenarios, have appeared in indexed journals.

PROLOGUE

The path of "returning to ...", commenced by Foucault and trod by Lacan in his reading of Freud, has become an essential method of carrying out research in the field of psychoanalysis.

By the mere fact that it sets out on this same path, this book by Miguel Gutiérrez-Peláez ensures a surprising rediscovery of Sándor Ferenczi. The author undertakes a retroactive reading of this rebellious disciple-analysand of Freud, subtly using the tools inherited from Lacan; and he amazes us with his findings of what was there, beneath the guise of an absence. This is undoubtedly a courageous venture, but in the case of *Confusion of Tongues: A Return to Sándor Ferenczi*, a totally justified and rigorously productive one.

One of the achievements of this singular book is, in my view, to have highlighted the destiny of repression, and even scorn, suffered by Ferenczi's oeuvre throughout the history of psychoanalysis (let us recall the disdain and even suspicion of psychosis disseminated by E. Jones); another is to have discovered the true reason for this discredit, that is, the rejection of the subversive value of inflammatory work about the numbed way in which psychoanalysis and its practice is presented, a new outlook that has permitted analysts to feel a kind of "warm comfort", totally foreign to Freudian ethics.

In this regard, the book that you are holding could not belong to any "history of psychoanalysis"; on the contrary, it is very contemporary, as will be any work that applies, without concession, the method defined by Lacan as "rethinking" (his particular way of returning to Freud). Of course, this must be pertinently done, dealing with a work that, like the Sileni, might still hide an *agalma*.

This is precisely what Miguel Gutiérrez-Peláez does in each chapter, as he delves not only into Ferenczi's heteroclite work but into many others, which he avails himself of in order to support and enrich his book. But this text also leads us into the field of clinical experience. Ferenczi's denunciation becomes a voice in the wilderness, as he exposes the most controversial issues of practice and its deviations. This is particularly relevant with regard to the "responsibility of the analyst", a phrase not devoid of moralism, which he uses to refer to the key place the "analyst's desire" occupies in the cure.

All of Ferenczi's work, Gutiérrez-Peláez warns us, is an insistent claim on the "awakening" of analysts. But there is a neglected fold among its texts: the one that makes of the function of language the crucial instance for the construction of the unconscious in childhood and for certain vicissitudes of the neurotic's particular history that will lead him to the couch. At this stage the entire journey of this provocative text is fully displayed.

Employing "Confusion of tongues between adults and the child", a paper presented by Ferenczi a year before his death in 1933, the text becomes a true "symbolic reduction" that functions like an open door: on the one hand, to the traumatic effects of language, always received by the *infans* as a "foreign language", due to the libidinal overload of *lalangue*; and, on the other, to a magnificent landscape of ideas, authors, and unique articulations, which Nicolás Casullo would have described as "the debate of ideas".

If the confines frequented and explored by Ferenczi are of interest to the "psychoanalytical movement" and not to the history of psychoanalysis, it is because they serve as a guide to the great topics of the practice. There is nothing more powerful than Ferenczi's "activism" and his audacity in demonstrating the fecundity of the deviation, and the insistence of truth in the mistake, when, regardless of the passion at play, there is an analyst who works according to the rules of the unconscious.

The propositions of his vast and diverse work (there is no theme present in it that does not interest psychoanalysis)—in his *Clinical Diary*, for example—are almost a testament, distilling a near-magical naivety; nevertheless, these are relevant, and even anticipatory, key issues, which Lacan will rescue from oblivion thirty years later, in order to raise them to the category of crucial problems for psychoanalysis. These questions arise in connection with the analyst's desire, and its validity, in the effectiveness of the cure; the limits of transference and the analyst's responsibility ("my students have inherited the mania of searching for the fault in themselves"); the problem of when to end the cure ("cure finishing": accommodating to what can be achieved and giving up the impossible or the highly improbable); and, *in extremis*, the concern for the consequences of the practice over the life and drive tendencies of the analyst. "Who is the madman, the patients or us?" is the heading for the diary entry dated 1 May 1932.

Concerning the question: "Who analyses?", it is evident that Ferenczi is limited to answering: "I do"—mistakes turn his diary into a personal document, an intimate confession of the extreme subjective implication of himself as practitioner. The absence of symbolic constraints in the relationship with his patients announces a tragi-comic outcome hanging over the scene ("I'm responsible for transference becoming so passionate, *due to my cold feelings*: promising sensations of preliminary pleasure which awaken hope, and then not giving anything"). The need to be "sensitive" will set in motion, practically at the end of his life, the "mutuality" of analysis, a technique based on the exacerbation of imaginary relationships with patients, and which will finally lead—at least in the case of an American patient—to a mutual telepathic cure across the ocean: a "technique" at which Ferenczi arrives attracted by the vertigo of the real. But he also takes his commitment to the analysand to its limits, questioning himself about "the complications arising from having more than one patient in analysis" (31 March 1932).

The effect of this book is that Ferenczi has returned: something we knew from our readings of Lacan, where multiple references about his work abound, informing us of his clinical importance, as well as from the myriad of publications, theses, and international congresses dedicated to him.

If there is something that Miguel Gutiérrez-Peláez clearly demonstrates it is that when post-Freudians were "on their way to", or, even better, "got away from", the Freudian essence, Ferenczi, even with his diversions and technical audacities (headaches for Freud), was "on his way back", bringing us the Freudian spirit and substance, sinking his blade into the most resisted but most pressing psychoanalytical questions of his day, and, also, of today. He was, without doubt, the first to place the analyst, rather than the analysand, in the dock.

For all these reasons, the task successfully undertaken by Miguel Gutiérrez-Peláez is by no means an ineffective one: rethinking Ferenczi's work from a contemporary perspective, where the problems of clinical practice are precisely those that Ferenczi was able to anticipate as being among the significant issues of psychoanalysis.

If, in our clinical work, we make experience out of "the bone of the real", that bone is continuously gnawed by the clinical practice that Ferenczi invented, defended with passion, and heartily wished Freud to approve of … without success.

Undoubtedly, Freud clearly understood that Ferenczi's *furor curandis* led him to many dead ends: "… Isn't Ferenczi a true cause for worry? Once again we have had no news of him for months. He feels offended because one is not delighted to know that he is playing the game of mother and son with his feminine patients." Nevertheless, he must have found something of value in his disciple's outbursts since, apart from calling him "my dear son", he also said of him: "Hungary, so close to Austria geographically and so distanced scientifically, up to now has offered psychoanalysis only one collaborator, S. Ferenczi; but such a one that he is worth an entire society."

Lacan, in his "Direction of the treatment …" said that the texts of Freud's "grand vizier" were "burning brands that will soon be ashes"; this valuable book that you are about to read is a strong gust of wind that comes to fan the flames that lie beneath the pages of the martyr of the unconscious that was Sándor Ferenczi.

Héctor López

CHAPTER ONE

Unveiling Ferenczi

"It is the courage of making a clean breast of it in face of every question that makes the philosopher. He must be like Sophocles' Oedipus, who, seeking enlightenment concerning his terrible fate, pursues his inde-fatigable enquiry, even when he divines that appalling horror awaits him in the answer. But most of us carry in our hearts the Jocasta, who begs Oedipus for God's sake not to enquire further; and we give way to her, and that is the reason why philosophy stands where it does."
Letter from Schopenhauer to Goethe (1815), cited by Ferenczi
(1912, italics in original)

Sándor Ferenczi's work has, after years of exclusion from the psychoan-alytic movement, returned in the same way in which what is repressed returns. It has been either forgotten or tainted as psychopathologic, anti-technical, anti-theoretical, anti-psychoanalytical—processes that have undoubtedly failed as defensive mechanisms. His work is back on stage and has resulted in various articles, studies, and revisions. Unfortunately, however, the new perspective on Ferenczi's work, rather than shedding light, covers with new veils the *real* that insists within it. Ferenczi's technical innovations, his eccentric patients, and his passion-ate relationship with Freud manage to dominate the entire spectrum

1

of these new studies and, thereby, the fundamental aspects of his work are once again concealed. Thus, Ferenczi's return has taken the form of a *reveiling*: it appears, only to become hidden once again. To recover that essential, nodal, aspect that insists and persists in Ferenczi's work, an *unveiling* is necessary that will, through a profound analysis of his oeuvre, make his return, as truth, possible.

Ferenczi can be placed, in the psychoanalytic movement, on the side of awakening. Therefore, a new reading of his work cannot be undertaken by returning it to sleep and sameness. His technical innovations, in accordance with his theoretical advances and clinical incursions, aim at producing a discomfort in the patient that goes against that natural movement of analysis towards sleep, thus producing an awakening. However, it so happens that papers and investigations of his work are not always compatible with that Ferenczian pledge to *dehypnotise*. It is therefore necessary to undertake a new reading that will rescue his importance for contemporary psychoanalysis.

It is important not to lose sight of the fact that this Ferenczian quest for awakening does not cease to be Freudian, since Freud is interested in the world of dreams, not because he wants to submerge in the obscure caverns of Morpheus (dark surgery, obscure analyst, obscure words), but rather, in fact, because of what that world contains of awakening. Freud knew that through the device of analysis, it isn't that the analysand finds his essence, the definite core of his being, the gold nugget that is put together in the composition of his cosmos; instead, he discovers that point in which his existence is torn, where the continuity of his life is broken, the gap that separates every attempt at wholeness of being with his own self from that *no-place* that confronts existence against its own fracture.

Undoubtedly, Ferenczi's richest writings are the ones he undertook during his last years. These works, particularly those written in 1932, are the most original and most distant from Freud's work. Despite their novelty, they nonetheless maintain a profound thread with the rest of his work and with the topics that summoned his interest from the start of his medical and psychoanalytic activities. Topics such as hypnosis and dehypnotising, technical innovations, work with "difficult" patients, the articulation between trauma and the traumatic, sexuality and language, the termination of analysis, among others, are questions that, to a greater or lesser extent, are present from his first writings, whether openly enunciated or in a germinal state that will come to light and bear fruit in his later work. Haynal (1997) points out how Ferenczi's essential interests are present in his pre-analytic writings. According to Haynal, these interests are: communication in its most hidden forms (Ferenczi, 1899); hypnosis (1904) and communication in love (1901); sexuality in its strangest manifestations (1902); and childhood (1904, 1908, 1913a, & 1913b). Regarding the latter, it is important to highlight that Ferenczi was not a child psychoanalyst (not even young Arpad was a patient of his) and, therefore, the concept of *childhood* enjoys fundamental nuance that needs to be specified. Such a notion of childhood is present in "The adaptation of the family to the child" (1928) and finally in "The confusion of tongues between adults and the child (The language of tenderness and of passion)" (1932a). For Haynal, such a childhood has nothing to do with innocence, but with *authenticity*, a trait that he rescues, along with Ferenczi; nevertheless, it is necessary to keep in mind that even if childhood *is* related to innocence, it is so only in relation to an innocence that is always lost, mythical, and structural.

In Ferenczi's writings of 1932 in particular, it is possible to find the root of what will be the greatest of post-Freudian discoveries: the apparatus of language, in its unconscious dimension, elaborated *a posteriori* in the work of Jacques Lacan. In Ferenczi, the traumatic dimension of language—in its double aspect: as the possibility of entrance into language and as a *destructuring* trauma, by the silencing of the subject through the imposition of the Other's word—acquires a description with biblical resonance: it is a *confusion of tongues*.

In "Confusion of tongues between adults and the child" (1932a) Ferenczi addresses this topic, of the traumatic dimension of language, with insistence; he poses the relationship between what he calls the tender language of the child and the passionate language of the adult. These two languages will be confronted, giving rise to trauma. That is where the "confusion of tongues" arises. This opens up the dimension of desire, because it is towards the language of the adult that the desire of the child is headed and where its dimension of meaning is disrupted. With Ferenczi, it is possible to rescue a notion of childhood from a hypothetical place, always lost, which is a place of the innocence of the child: a state previous to *passionality*, injected by language and by the articulation of desire with language. Childhood, in his writings, belongs to what is *unblotted*, paradisiacal, but it is necessary to read that childhood from its structural place, from its permanently lost dimension, since an immaculate childhood is undoubtedly an untenable notion from the point of view of psychoanalysis, which considers the infant as desiring and polymorphously perverse. The confusion of tongues, therefore, like the *real* dimension of language, is, on the one hand, structuring and inevitable in so far as it makes possible the acquisition of the word, but, on the other, makes reference to trauma, such as clinical trauma, when what takes place is not the delivery of the word but the silencing of the voice by the imposition of the Other's voice. The other traumatic situations that Ferenczi alludes to, set off by the "passionality" of the adult, come from this initial traumatic dimension.

A thorough and unprejudiced reading of Ferenczi's work cannot ignore the fact that the Hungarian psychoanalyst does not emerge from his struggles undefeated, and, to a certain extent, does not end up taking the steps that he himself proposes. It is later, through Lacan's work, that those pioneering steps are taken and the dimension of language is opened up entirely. Ferenczi thinks of the encounter with the real, with that real that is the confusion of tongues—accidental and inevitable, which is the possibility of the emergence of the word and, at the same time, the impossibility for every speaker—as an encounter with reality, that is, with the imaginary reality that governs human beings. Freud was deeply annoyed with this and criticised him for believing to be real that which occurs in fantasy, for confusing the events of the world with the fantasies of the neurotic. As the reality of historical events demonstrated, Freud and Ferenczi could not escape the fact that the appearance of the confusion of tongues came between them. Freud's critique of Ferenczi's presentation with respect to the "confusion of tongues" is undoubtedly mistaken: he fails to interpret the fact that in the controversial writings of his disciple and colleague there is no return to the initial and old-fashioned conceptions of psychoanalysis, but rather a return of the real of language that appeared as if untouched by analytic practice itself. The trauma that Ferenczi places in reality, a product of the perverse operations of human beings, is a "real" that cuts across every speaker; his insertion in language as inclusion in the Other's desire, the unfathomable core of speech practice itself.

It is in this manner that Ferenczi confronts himself in his practice with a "real". Psychoanalysts of his time were clever enough to avoid this real, circumventing it so as not to see it, to make it disappear from the scene (the scene is always, by definition, an attempt to exclude the real), and in that way they led the natural movement of analysis towards sleep. They employed the same mechanism with the real that they afterwards employed with Ferenczi and his work. But, once again, what lay repressed made its way through. The real that Ferenczi ultimately did not know what to do with, that he tried to give meaning to, finding a place in analysis for it by means of technical innovations, is none other than the real of the dimension of language itself, precisely the dimension that he refers to as the *confusion of tongues*.

Ferenczi does not extend himself over the nature of that confusion of tongues. He doesn't seem to offer explanations beyond the setting up in conflict of two languages: that of the child and of the adult, the language of tenderness and the language of passion. Nevertheless, when Ferenczi stops there, in the figure of the father and the son, the teacher and the disciple, the analyst and the analysand, he inevitably opens up a wound across the entire analytic discipline: the traumatic dimension of language. That point of unsuturability is, for Ferenczi, the nodal point that structures Freudian discovery, which Lacan will try to address from different angles through the complexity of his practice and his thought (including the concepts of *lalangue* and *troumatisme*), and which is still how psychoanalysis, and what precisely occurs during analytic practice, can be understood. Ferenczi recognises the numbness produced by psychoanalysis and aims at an awakening, an awakening to a real that operates, constantly, outside of all speech.

It is necessary, therefore, to set in motion an investigation that will delve into Ferenczi's work in order to listen to what is spoken within it about that real. During the past few years, interest in Ferenczi's work has revived but, unfortunately, it has generally been read from a post-Freudian perspective, disregarding the originality of his work, whose fundamental aspects remain, for this reason, hidden. Ferenczi's work is generally read in three main ways: as an antecedent of technical variation (validating, beginning with Ferenczi, the production of changes within the psychoanalytic framework); as the work of a dissident of psychoanalysis who rebels against Freudian orthodoxy; and as a foundation from which to think about trauma as something truthful, beyond psychic reality, as a fact of material reality. Nevertheless, it would seem that what returns again and again in Ferenczi's work has not found its true place but has always remained trapped in the figure of the disguise. Thus, in the interest of unveiling its content, his work becomes tainted by the words of others or it is used as a precedent to someone else's concepts. But the real that insists and persists in his work would appear to be unable, in each disclosure, to avoid the new form that conceals it.

How can we avoid falling into this trap? How can we not become victims of what is being denounced here? How can an oeuvre speak with its own voice, with its mother tongue, or is it that even the mother tongue is always in the place of foreignness; is the mother tongue always the voice of the other? How can we rescue the subject who speaks with those voices of the other? Surely, by proceeding with caution. Falling down dead in the entrails of one's own inventions cannot be a destiny. Daedalus managed to escape from Crete's labyrinth, which he himself had built for the gods. He had the humility his son lacked.

As Héctor López (1994) correctly points out, the psychoanalytic movement is not the same as the history of psychoanalysis. The latter is composed of the contingencies of the historical timescale that determines a chronology of events according to a "before" and an "after". The former, on the other hand, is connected not by time but by the logic that makes of the heteroclite dimensions of psychoanalysis one same body. This difference explains why certain authors, who belonged to the history of psychoanalysis, did not form part of its movement. Adler and Jung are excluded from the psychoanalytic movement not because of a whim on Freud's part but because their works, according to their own logic, are outside of the conceptual structure of psychoanalysis. The turns of Freudian thought serve as evidence that he moved by the logic of that which he was discovering and investigating (the unconscious) and not because of the desire to find proof and conclusions made *a priori*. Freud wished to place himself as a man of modernity, but his loyalty to the psychoanalytic movement meant that he ran into the modern project's own breakdown.

López places psychoanalytic discourse as a movement that goes from an S1 Freud to an S2 Lacan, this S2 being a moment of retro-foundation of psychoanalysis in which a metaphor is produced in the march across the significant chain that is the history of psychoanalysis. In this series of movements, histories, and discourses, what place does Sándor Ferenczi have? Undoubtedly, he lies within the psychoanalytic movement, since his work is coherent with the logic that structures it. In our view, the readings that have been made of his work would place him as yet another link within the metonymy of the significant chain. We consider that a modern reading of Ferenczi's oeuvre allows us to re-signify (make a metaphor of) his place within the psychoanalytic movement, not as a museum piece, fixed in a past period of psychoanalysis, but as a production that will provide answers and generate questions for the future of psychoanalysis. Ferenczi, like Freud, followed the path of the unconscious to such an extent that some of his contemporaries felt he was diverging from the logic of psychoanalysis, without understanding that the movement of the unconscious itself was charting the course. Today, many decades after his death, we find in Ferenczi's work a validity that has not yet been studied, that is raw and undigested. It is necessary, therefore, to produce a reading that will bring to light the originality and relevance that, despite the many readings and studies undertaken, has still been left in the shadows.

It is important to keep in mind, despite the timelessness of the unconscious, the time in which we find ourselves today. Perhaps the return to Ferenczi is possible because through Lacan there has already been a return to Freud, and that without that earlier movement, what we now propose would not find its way. Elements, concepts, signifiers, elaborations, and awakening would be missing. As López (2007) suggests, taking up Lacan once more, the reading—and the research—consists in placing the diachrony of the concepts in synchrony with the work. In this regard, Lacan's work helps us to conceptually place the synchronic axis of Ferenczi's work in the metonymic diachrony of his production.

The history of psychoanalysis wanted to forget the scars left by Ferenczi, cover up with fine cloths the cuts made on his skin, but under the jet of water of his historiography and his theories, they found themselves, like Lady Macbeth, indelibly stained. Ferenczi, in his devotion to psychoanalysis and the unconscious, ended up like those Messiahs that act like heretics within religion—like Saint Francis of Assisi, Sor Juana Inés de la Cruz, or Shabbetai Zevi. It is worth remembering the words of the famous Gershom Sholem, great friend of Walter Benjamin and brilliant scholar of the Kabbalah in the twentieth century, who affirms that

> Judaism, like a genuine religious tradition, only saves itself precisely where it lets heresies flow. Heresies constantly renew great religious experiences. Actually, one of the great paradoxes of great religious traditions is that the mystics ... are those who simultaneously represent tradition, in a radical and powerful sense, but they probe tradition in such a way that they take it to its limits, they are subversives of tradition itself in their quest to radically affirm it. (Cited by Forster, 2006)

The apparently absurd place attained by Ferenczian technical innovation does not lie outside of psychoanalysis, a deviation of its ontological premises, but is the logical consequence of its own movement.

Ferenczi operates therefore like an *antinomist*, that is, one going against the *nomos*, the law. But this is not an attempt to go against those traditions that have given consistency to certain beliefs or to science; on the contrary: what is expressed is absolute loyalty to those traditions, to the extent that such loyalty makes the fibres that have produced them, and given them consistency, stumble. There lies the horror that Ferenczi produces in the history of the psychoanalytic movement. He lays bare, once again, the fact that heresy is a logical consequence of power structures; that the same logic that is established to preserve the legitimacy of the structures and institutions produces, in one same (Möbian) movement, its (apparently) contrary result. The revolution, within the very logic of its process, and not in its deviation, tends to reproduce the mechanisms against which it revolts. In turn, the strengthening of orthodoxy and faith ends up shaking the foundations under which a coagulated knowledge rests. For this reason, we do not consider Ferenczi a revolutionary but a subversive. The present study aims at throwing light on the traumatic dimension of language as a *confusion of tongues*—an aspect that even today remains hidden in Sándor Ferenczi's oeuvre—thus allowing us to show its relevance for contemporary psychoanalysis.

CHAPTER TWO

In the terrain of trauma

"The immediate effect of a trauma which cannot be dealt with at once is fragmentation."

"Notes and fragments (1930)",
(Ferenczi, 1932c, p. 230)

"*Anxiety* is the direct sequel of each trauma."

"Notes and fragments (1931)",
(Ferenczi, 1932c, p. 249, italics in original)

In a chapter of his book *El porvenir del inconsciente* (The future of the unconscious) (2006), Jorge Alemán makes the strange assertion that Lacan's late teaching is no longer psychoanalysis. However, he does not explain what he means but rather leaves that task to future generations. He affirms, in an interview granted to Emilia Cueto and published in *Imago Agenda* that

> Lacan, like every great thinker, exceeds the genre by means of which he made his way. What is excellent always exceeds the genre but doesn't make it relative. The farther he arrives with psychoanalysis, he can, also through psychoanalysis, give rise to a supplement

without nomination which, so as not to extend myself, I would say
it's a new type of writing, sexed and mortal, about the speaker's
condition. (Cueto, 2006, p. 40)

This is an enquiry about the limits of psychoanalysis, the frontier that is
woven, the "ins" and "outs" of the field. In a similar fashion, Ferenczi
will insert the question about the limits of psychoanalysis into analytic
discipline. In a similar, not a contrary, movement, Ferenczi provokes a
rumbling from the scaffolding upon which psychoanalysis is built. His
own devotion to the psychoanalytic movement and to the discovery of
the unconscious leads him to confront the totality of the movement as
to the limits of its freedom.

In this regard, it is possible to affirm that Ferenczi's place in the history
of the psychoanalytic movement is traumatic. But, what is the nature of
that trauma? Or, better still, what is trauma? The question about trauma
is precisely what creates the breaking point between those two great
thinkers of the first generation of analysts: Freud and Ferenczi.

We have asked: "What is trauma?", but the *what* is never innocent
and, perhaps, that way of asking about things that Heidegger (1955)
managed to denounce is what veils the appearance of the essential with
regard to trauma. Nevertheless, this *what*, at least for now, seems impossible to avoid and demands attention, even if only as a fictional tool
with which to place a series of important cards on the table.

With Sigmund Freud

Roudinesco and Plon (1998), by distinguishing trauma from traumatism, bring to light a preciseness that, at least in the first instance,
seems important. Thus, traumatism is understood to be the contingent
event that produces psychic effects, and trauma is the effect of that
contingency on the person exposed to the traumatism. This distinction
undoubtedly appears in Freud's own writings, from where such
definitions can be traced. Freud's thinking starts to take shape with his
writings about trauma, his famous "traumatic" theory, and the traumatic effects of seduction on illness and the appearance of symptoms.
Contingent events in reality, such as seduction and sexual abuse, have
traumatic effects that become hidden in the unconscious due to repression, maintaining silence as long as the state of affairs, in apparent equi-
librium, are not altered. Nevertheless, later on, something apparently

unconnected to that repressed trauma takes place, and the unconscious, silent but on the lookout, manages to weave unexpected nets, availing itself of its own symbolic resources, of certain significant and meaningful sets of logic. When this second moment or second scene takes place (*Nachträglichkeit*), given the respective associations, the previous trauma regains significance, and the hidden trauma in the unconscious reappears, with its consequent range of symptoms. The treatment, therefore, consists in reconstructing the threads that link this second moment with the first and which have fallen into oblivion. The remembrance via analysis will therefore be the path that will lift the repression and put an end to the symptoms.

Nevertheless, Freud will give a turn to his theory whose effects will be catastrophic for many analysts (see Chapter Five). He will sense that in his patients' narratives about sexual trauma there is a persistence of scenes that in no way can have their correlate in reality, since this would lead to an exponential growth of cases of abuse, of the production of obsessive neurosis, perversion, and hysteria that does not correspond with the evidence in reality. Consequently, he will announce in a letter to Wilhelm Fliess, in an often cited phrase, that "I no longer believe in my *neurotica* [theory of the neuroses]" (1897e, p. 259), referring to the weak foundations of his theory since, whether on purpose or not, his patients had lied to him: they had narrated, as real, events that were products of their neurotic fantasies. In this way, the concept of psychic reality, partly in contrast to real occurrences, will appear. And in this abandonment of the theory of trauma, psychoanalysis as such makes its appearance, going beyond the therapeutics of memory.

However, this is not the end of the theorisation of trauma. With the turn Freud's thinking takes in 1920, and with the possibility of isolating the function of the death drive, Freud will be able to go beyond the pleasure principle; studying the effects of war traumas on oneiric reality and the persistence of displeasure will reveal that it is not the pleasure principle that reigns hegemonic in the psychic system. Along the same lines, in an article entitled "Constructing the truth: From 'Confusion of tongues' to 'Constructions in analysis'", Jaques Press (2006) presents a definition of trauma on the basis of a quotation from Assmann (1997), according to which it is only through a given framework "'that a [traumatic] event becomes experienceable, communicable and memorable'" (p. 26, cited by Press, p. 528). In psychoanalytic terms, trauma is understood as that which lacks a possible frontier to embody a specific experience. Inasmuch as it transcends all possible frames, the experience becomes *inexperienceable*, that is, it is devoid of representation and, therefore, impossible to remember, its footprint insistent in the psychic system in the form of repetition.

When Freud acquaints himself with the paper Ferenczi wants to present at the Wiesbaden Congress in 1932, he will find a phantom he thought had long been buried. He will read in Ferenczi's considerations his own thoughts that had been buried since the beginning of the century. But Ferenczi was not digging up a corpse or, if he was, it was not with the purpose of bringing to life an "old" Freud, or at least not the one that the Freud of 1932 thought he had found in that paper. Ferenczi brought something up from the dungeons; something hidden in the discourse and symptomatology of his patients and hidden, also, between the lines in the theoretical work of the analysts of his day and of Freud himself. As analytic thought advanced along new paths, making progress and questioning the facts, Ferenczi wrote about something that did not appear explicitly but rather in the blank spaces between words, between phrases, and which was the real that insisted not only in his clinical practice but in his thinking and his writings. It was thus that he brought to the analytic scene a real that was there at the start of Freud's thinking, and only in that sense is it a return. Rather than Ferenczi's being a return to an "old" Freud, it is a return of the repressed within psychoanalytic thinking and psychoanalytic practice itself. It is possible to understand, in the manner in which Freud reacted to this paper (the correspondence between Jones and others is proof of this), that Freud read this return through the frame of mind of his early years of analytic investigation regarding traumatic theory. However, what Ferenczi was now producing, and which has so often been read through that Freudian filter, was something entirely different; something more fundamental, more primitive and primary, and of such complexity that it involves the totality of psychoanalytic thought and of the limits of language as the frontier of its practice.

With Sándor Ferenczi

In his last years, Ferenczi involves himself in the intense work of theoretical writing about trauma. Testimony of that work is his "Confusion of tongues between adults and the child" (1932a), his *Clinical Diary* (1932b) written in 1932, his notes, published posthumously under the title "Notes and fragments" (1932c), and a separate brief paper published as "Reflections on trauma"[1] (1934). The thematic focus in these writings is on developing ideas about traumatism and the psychic mechanisms that intervene into, rather than complete, theories. His writings convey questioning and conjecture, daring and meticulous probing. He tries, with the means at his disposal, to express that which appears on his couch through his sick patients.

In "Confusion of tongues between adults and the child" (1932a), Ferenczi sets out to broaden the topic of the exterior origin of trauma and its influence on character and neuroses, rescuing the role of the traumatic factor—which he considers has been put aside in psychoanalytic theory—in an apparent return to some previous concepts of Freudian formulation. Nevertheless, as will be pointed out throughout this investigation, at that point where Ferenczi seems to resort to a return to the initial concepts of psychoanalysis, in particular to Freud's first theories of trauma, what actually returns is a real that has been excluded from clinical analytic work; precisely at the point where a way back seems possible, like Ulysses' ancient *nostos*, what we find is a push towards the frontier, towards the limits of analytic practice itself, towards that which Alemán (2000) has brilliantly termed the threshold between sense and drive.

In the article Ferenczi distinguishes between two love tendencies: the tender and the erotic; the child, psychically, affectively, and biologically is affected by the former, and the latter is (at best) the adult's domain. Nevertheless, certain adults with psychopathologic predispositions confuse the tender language of the child with the sexual desires of a mature person and let themselves be driven by these without considering the consequences. The title of the article refers precisely to this, giving rise to the confusion of tongues incurred by the adult with respect to what the child manifests. The child, in turn, cannot always defend himself against this nor manifest his rejection, becoming paralysed by intense fear and, more specifically:

> The same anxiety, however, if it reaches a certain maximum, compels them to subordinate themselves like automata to the will of the aggressor, to divine each one of his desires and to gratify these; completely oblivious of themselves they identify themselves with the aggressor. Through the identification, or let us say, introjection of the aggressor, he disappears as part of the external reality, and becomes intra- instead of extra-psychic … the

attack as a rigid external reality ceases to exist and in the traumatic
trance the child succeeds in maintaining the previous situation of
tenderness. (Ferenczi, 1932a, p. 228, italics in original)

In this way, the child introjects the adult feelings of guilt. After the sexual
act, after the sexual abuse to which the adult subjects the child, what
previously appeared to the child to be a game turns him into someone
who deserves to be punished. Trying to recover from the aggression,
the child finds himself split, being guilty as well as innocent; the links
with his own feelings, perceptions, and senses having been destroyed,
he lapses into a state of confusion. In this way, the child does not defend
himself but becomes identified with the aggressor and introjects what
appears to him as threatening. Thus, in the child's reaction, the split in
the personality is announced. In other texts, Ferenczi (1929) works on
the idea of how the child confronts himself with a great fear if he is pre-
maturely stimulated in his genital sensations, since his desire goes hand
in hand not with the violent passion of the adult but with play and the
demonstration of tender feelings.

At this stage, the secret schemes by which the confusion of tongues
exerts its power start to unfold. Desire is the desire of the other insofar
as the other is the one that speaks. The child speaks through him and is
spoken by him. The adult's words, which have never been external in
the way that the differentiation of an inside and an outside can be external, speak through the child, and for the child those words are his own
voice. In this regard, the extent to which the mother tongue is always a
foreign tongue becomes more evident. Perhaps the experience of psychoanalysis is not alone in being able to return those voices to their
exterior place, their "outsideness", but only in this experience can the
logic of how these mechanisms work be found. The word itself, given
this relationship between the child's voice and that of the adult, always
gains the place of confusion, of one over the other, of silencing the one
so that the other can impose itself. This is the violence of the word and
the dominant power of language. It seems that there is no possible dia-
lectic that can resolve this confusion of tongues.

Ferenczi distinguishes three potentially traumatic situations: inces-
tuous seduction, passionate punishment, and the terrorism of suffering. Due to the effect of trauma, the psychic apparatus fragments
itself and the possibilities of remembering traumatic events begin to
erase themselves. In this way, the child lacks the mechanisms to link

the excess of excitation: he is invaded by over-excitation against which he can impose no barrier or veil. Ferenczi finds the traumatic factor a universal and considers that the analysis cannot be considered finished while the material is not reached; it is, initially, accessible by repetition but not, given its experiential character, by remembrance.

Towards the end of "Confusion of tongues between adults and the child", Ferenczi attempts to outline more precisely what happens at the psychic level, starting from the traumatic experience. He affirms that

> [if] the shocks increase in number during the development of the child, the number and the various kinds of splits in the personality increase too, and soon it becomes extremely difficult to maintain contact without confusion with all the fragments, each of which behaves as a separate personality yet does not know of even the existence of the others. Eventually it may arrive at a state which— continuing the picture of *fragmentation*—one would be justified in calling *atomization*. One must possess a good deal of optimism not to lose courage when facing such a state, though I hope even here to be able to find threads that can link up the various parts. (1932a, p. 229, italics in original)

This quotation reveals even more clearly the situation that causes Ferenczi's collision with the material presented by his patients. The defence mechanism can result in the division of the psyche into various parts, depending on the incidence and intensity of the traumatisms to which the child is exposed. He suggests the term *atomisation* (*Atomisierung*) as a cautionary measure with respect to another, *fragmentation* (*Fragmentierung*), but which would seem more in line with what clinical practice evinces. At this point, a light is shed on the way in which this idea begins to take shape in his writings.

What sense can be made of the proliferation of signifiers and of colourful language in Ferenczi's writings? Undoubtedly, what is at play there is an attempt to catch something, that "there is" that questions him like a Levinasian face that says to him: "Here I am." Ferenczi tries to give it meaning and, in order to do so, resorts to the scientific elements he has to hand, but perhaps loyalty to that which insists there, serving as his motor and his passion, does not completely close him in a theoretical totality, rather leaves the space open, stalking him from one side to the other. He continues trying to find its basis in reality, in the seductive event that really took place; but if the discussion were to end there, if what was there was nothing more than the effects of a perverse and abusive adult acting in psychic integrity, we would be doing to Ferenczi's work that which he tried to resist and which he disagreed with: silencing that real in a totality, by producing its concealment with a conceptualisation disguised as controversial, soaking it with signifiers that prevent hearing something about the real that makes its appearance in his clinical experience and in his writings.

Ferenczi explains in "Confusion of tongues ..." how the adult uses the child for his drive satisfaction, whether it be sexual or emotional (of anger or hatred). This behaviour of the adult takes the child unaware. The traumatic event begins to destroy what was a previous state of security with respect to the world around the child: someone who previously conveyed feelings of trust to the child now leads him into a state of total helplessness, and the traumatised subject is now overwhelmed by a feeling of total insecurity. As a result, the child subjects himself to the adult and begins to identify with the perpetrator, managing to make the aggression itself disappear from exterior reality, maintaining, in this way, the situation of tenderness that reigned before trauma barged in. Nevertheless, Ferenczi tells us, this is not sufficient to constitute trauma and, just as in Freud's elaboration of trauma, a second moment is required, which in this case is the adult's response. Ferenczi considers there to be two stages in the pathologisation of trauma; the traumatic situation alone does not necessarily result in the generation of trauma. There is a second phase that has to do with the lack of support from those on whom the child depends. With regard to second stage, we observe that "the mother's disapproval as a dysfunction of the word is a traumatic agent that redoubles precocious initiations, which are dysfunctions of the child's libido" (Sabourin, 1984, p. 19). The behaviour of the adult with respect to the abused child is directly related to the psychic mechanism that is at play in the crystallisation of trauma.

Ferenczi's theory of trauma becomes complex when he comes to consider the effects of memory and of remembering. The reaction produced by trauma is a break with reality, generating the *self-destruction of conscience*. Thought and perception come to a halt, paralysing the psychic functions, and no possible record of these impressions is possible, not even at the unconscious level. Consequently, it is impossible to remember what has happened. The psychic system does not retain any of the traumatic impressions. Having no record and, consequently, no possibility of remembrance or of this material coming into consciousness, it becomes clear that what is at play has nothing to do with repression but is related to a mythical and structural dimension. Many of Ferenczi's readers will suggest that generally a trauma occurs during early childhood, but, although it has its place in reality, it somehow never becomes conscious. However, that immaculate childhood aims at a structural dimension that has to do with the trauma immersed in a sea of words, something that has hardly been considered.

The psyche, by identifying itself with the person who committed the aggression, guarantees its own existence, thus finding a means of surviving the abuse. In this way, the child is able to maintain the "good" image of the adult. These aggressions are serious: they are related to rape or punishment of passion; particularly, punishments due to faults that the child does not consider himself to have committed. Even so, the child finds it necessary to identify with the aggressor in order to maintain the good image of the adult (aggressor) that is so crucial for him. As a result of the split, the child becomes innocent and guilty at the same time. The adult, on the other hand, moved by remorse, denies what has taken place, thus increasing the effects of the trauma, producing the child's distrust in his own senses. Are we to understand that the child's guilt appears because he has lost his innocence, because of the dismemberment produced by the entrance of language, a shame brought about by the desiring and sexed body, namely, an Adamic guilt before the loss of *Ursprache* and eternity, as well as the entrance into history?

In "Reflections on trauma" (1934), a series of notes published posthumously, Ferenczi specifies the effects of traumatism on the psyche:

> Shock=annihilation of self-regard—of the ability to put up a resistance, and to act and think in defence of one's own self; perhaps even the *organs* which secure self-preservation give up their function or reduce it to a minimum. (The word *Erschütterung* is derived from *schütten*, i.e. to become "unfest, unsolid", to lose one's own form and to adopt easily and without resistance, an imposed form—"like a sack of flour"). (1955, pp. 253–254)

The person abandons himself before the traumatic situation. Subjectivity is ruined, there is a destruction of the person and total surrender to that other who has committed the aggression.

Once again, Ferenczi discovers in his clinical work how trauma, as the confusion of tongues, leads to the silencing of the child's word by the imposition of the adult's, to the extent that the child's own voice and his own experience are erased and his reality denied. It is the other's reality that begins to operate as the measure of the world. The entrance into language occurs by erecting the difference of the other as an enemy of the same; the voice of the other, inasmuch as something different from me is the limit of language, the unnameable point, of the unmentionable word. When the other speaks, not like my other but like a radical otherness, the structure of language, as a communication mechanism that functions by circumscribing the whole to universal signifiers, is no longer possible. But the structure of language is precisely the structure of the inability to communicate, because it prevents the other from talking, from making radical otherness its appearance in the word. Undoubtedly, at this point it is necessary to befriend the poets: without ceasing to belong to the order of language, but, precisely by adopting it as a home, as an abode as well as battlefield, they manage to stretch the frontiers of language until its folds become transparent; taking the reader there, amidst those transparent folds they invite him to contemplate without too much ruthlessness the rays of light that appear on the other side. Ferenczi, in that same movement of pushing up against the ropes, exposes the psychoanalytic field to the limits of its own liberty; namely, the frontier that frames the character of a speaking and a sexed practice.

With Jacques Lacan

It is not easy to trace the presence of Ferenczi in Lacan's thinking. The fact that he appreciated him, that he used, recommended, and incorporated him, is well known; but tracing the presence of Ferenczi's thinking and the way in which Lacan uses it is difficult, as is the case with the majority of references in the work of the French psychoanalyst. We know, through Granoff (1997), that Lacan recommended he read Ferenczi. Barzilai (1997) suggests differences in understanding the concept of *Nachträglichkeit* on the part of both psychoanalysts. Going over Lacan's seminars, we can see that Ferenczi's name appears at certain crucial moments. Undoubtedly, there must have been identification, at some level, with respect to their place within psychoanalysis, of *enfant terrible,* and of being *excommunicated.* But perhaps the most effective, and less obvious connection, and the least studied, is the relationship of Ferenczi to language, and, in particular, the relationship between trauma and language in the confusion of tongues (Gutiérrez-Peláez, 2015).

André Haynal (1997) ventures to establish relationships between Ferenczi and Lacan. He affirms that, despite the worldwide exclusion of Ferenczi's oeuvre, Lacan openly expressed his interest in his work. It is worth remembering that, even in the United States, Ferenczi was not taught in psychoanalytic institutes. In England, his writings found more fertile ground thanks to Balint, in the Kleinian groups, and in Winnicott's "Middle Group". Lacan makes the following distinction in his "The direction of the treatment and the principles of its power" (1958): "… it can be said that Ferenczi's article, 'Introjection and trans- ference', dating from 1909, was inaugural, and it anticipated from afar all the themes later developed about the topic [of transference]" (p. 592). He continues with comments about Ferenczian thought: "Outside this hearth of the dispersed Hungarian school whose firebrands are now scattered and will soon be ashes, only the English with their cold objec- tivity have been able to articulate this gap to which the neurotic bears witness in wanting to justify his existence, and hence implicitly to dis- tinguish from the inter-human relation, with its warmth and its allure- ments, that relation to the Other in which being finds its status" (p. 593). But despite Haynal's attempt to establish a link between the French and the Hungarian analysts, it is not substantial enough to confirm a con- ceptual relationship.

The real that we are attempting to elucidate in Ferenczi perhaps finds its most adequate form in Lacan's last teaching, more precisely, in not placing any form before the real, in circumventing the image and expos- ing the face to that real. In a lecture about trauma, Eric Laurent (2002) cites Lacan: "The symptom is the subject's answer to the traumatic aspect of the real." Thus, the relationship between symptom as a mani- festation of illness, trauma, and the real is made evident. In this regard, we find in Lacan the fulcrums with which to make a new reading of Ferenczi that allows us to rediscover in him anticipation of the current issues in psychoanalysis as well as his ethical position as an analyst. On these foundations rests what is fundamental in Ferenczi's discov- ery, which usually remains hidden: that trauma does not correspond to a traumatism that occurred in reality, but to something that is struc- turally more profound, a response by the human and speaking subject confronted with the real. In this way, the contingent participation of reality in the operation of trauma—undoubtedly a leading role—is not avoided; instead, what is being affirmed is that the *traumatising* element of the traumatic situation does not lie in the events that took place—that is, in the imaginary account that can be made of it, or in the effects it can have on phantasmatic construction—but instead lies in what the account veils, which, once again, is the real as the threshold of the speaker's word.

That real, which insists and persists, finds a substitute for the voice that cannot be heard in the symptomatic manifestations of the sick patient. But technique will once again find there the nodal point that launches the question that governs and guides Ferenczian thinking: can what happens in that analysis go further than the confusion of tongues or is the confusion itself the limit of psychoanalysis as a practice of speech? Lacan, in turn, moves on the same grounds in what is known as his last teaching: how can the real be included in analytic practice without making of that real an image or a representation? How can the real be processed as real without reducing what insists in the real, starting from the silencing of the word at the symbolic level? Ferenczi enounces this in different ways, and an echo of his persistence is found in the thoughts of other authors, such as Donald D. Winnicott, for example: how can we avoid the analytic device repeating the initial scheme that produced the trauma?

To enrich this discussion, it is pertinent to include thinkers who come from other fields of knowledge; Walter Benjamin and Emmanuel Levinas, for example, are key figures. As thinkers within the Jewish tradition, they insert their philosophical reflections into what is essential about language and the written word. Their contributions to the topic of translation and the confusion of tongues are fitting in to a review of Ferenczi's work. Specifically, the topic of translation, discussed in this book, is not only appropriate because of the difficulties presented by the passage of Ferenczi's works from one language to another, but also because the very nature of language has led to his having been misunderstood.

With Walter Benjamin

Walter Benjamin, like most important twentieth-century Jewish philosophers, uses Judaism as a backdrop to all his thinking. For these philosophers, the promise of the figure of the future Messiah, as well as the meaning of the written word, have special weight. Benjamin, for his part, guided by his friend Gershom Sholem, delves into Kabalistic themes and the reading of the Torah; thus, his constant question regarding the status of language and the written word. The figure of Adam and its relation with nominative language, as the one who gives the precise name to those who inhabit Paradise, and the myth of the Tower of Babel as the birthplace of the confusion of tongues and all translation, will become central in his thinking. Reflecting on those biblical passages where the birth of history itself, through the expulsion of Adam and Eve from Paradise, is described, Benjamin will start to analyse in detail what it means to be a translator and what translation itself entails. He does not naively pretend to restore the place of a universal language, the famous *Ursprache* that reigned prior to all language, nor a *Grundsprache*, which wove a divine link like the one enjoyed by President Daniel Paul Schreber, but instead thinks of a *Zwischensprache* or *interlanguage*, one that is produced by, and flows in, the passage from the text of one language to another. In each of his translations, which are not transcriptions of texts from one language to another but the production of new texts, the contents of language are exploited and further enriched as new meanings are expressed. In this way, guided by the figure of the translator, Benjamin pretends to circumvent the confusion of tongues constitutive of each language, not by placing one language as superior to another, nor by giving more importance to the original over the translation, but by considering the *Zwischensprache* as the possibility of a coming together of language with its own semantic potential, as a place where written language comes face-to-face with its own self. It is in this opening, in this rupture, in the *in-between* of two languages, between one language and the other, that Benjamin finds what is fundamental to the experience of language. It is not the *entity* of the structure of language, its essence but, on the contrary, its *betweenness*, its place of transit, of opening, of rupture, of vanishing.

This dimension of *betweenness* is essential to articulate the relationship of Benjamin's philosophy with psychoanalysis, since what analysis aims at is not to rescue the original voice, the *Ursprache* of the analysand, the word from its essence (nor the essence from its word), nor to understand that the language imposed by the Other is the ultimate word that speaks within him. On the contrary, analysis tries to place the subject within the tension that constitutes him, against that lack in the place of fundamentals; and in the movement of that tension, and in the word that can be articulated from, and over, it, a language can be rescued that enables the subject to emerge from the alienation produced by being spoken by the Other and thus start to render an account of the analytic subject.

With Emmanuel Levinas

Levinas is one of the most important thinkers of the twentieth century and perhaps the philosopher who most seriously tried to think about difference, the difference, outside of the concept, that closes the universe of meaning into a totality, finding himself at the very limits of language, with the difficulty it presents in thinking about the other. Levinas centres his ethical thinking in the figure of the other and is extremely careful—and perhaps the totality (always open) of his work may be no more than an attempt to get around the problem, in order to circumvent the impossibility that he comes up against—to affirm the place of that other, not like the other of myself, but the other as such. In other words, he attempts to centre all the weight of his ethical reflections in that other, previous to all, *a priori*, without making a representation of it, without closing it in the field of sameness, but preserving, instead, its place as other and the radical difference of that other as a foundation without foundation, *an-archic* of all ethical reflection and of justice.

Levinas' appeal is motivated by his attempt to understand that radical other, preserving its *outsideness*, its *beyondness*, without enclosing it within the totalising frontiers of the concept. Levinas is essential insofar as he places that radical other in what can be named in this study as a "beyondness" of the confusion of tongues, in as much as it preserves its *outsideness*. The language of metaphysics, which turns words into concepts that enclose the multiplicity in the *one*, has not been able to think the other. The attempts to think through the difference, including the Derridian *différance*, end up thinking the other as the *other of*: the other of someone, the other of me. That way of understanding the different as different *from* something does not refrain from proposing *sameness* as the measure and starting point of the *other*. Levinas attempts to go beyond this, beyond that tendency of sameness characteristic of language and of philosophy.

In this way, Levinas places us within a core issue, since his way of using language, and of placing the radical other as the axis of philosophical thought, provides tools to think about that place of the other prior to the confusion of tongues, the place where Ferenczi's immaculate childhood is. As a result, there are two axes at play: the first relating to that real dimension of language, which, starting with Ferenczi, is enounced as a *confusion of tongues*, a place of impossibility, unwavering but always present as impossible to symbolise; and the second, the place of that mythical *other* that questions the possibility of a future prior to the confusion as an immaculate place, inasmuch as it has not been pierced by language, and is a foreigner to the word.

Having been able to trace this journey in Levinas, and without suggesting in any way a psychoanalysis inspired by him, we can proceed to insert this thought about the *other* as an issue of psychoanalysis: namely, how can that *other* be included in the analytic experience? How can analysis be open to the radical other and not a tendency towards sameness or difference of something? How can we conceive of difference as an analytic occurrence that appeals neither to an essential language nor to the recovery of an innocent and tender childhood? Placing reflection in openness to the other claims the advent and presence of an other that is not sameness as alienation of being by the other's word nor difference on the basis of the other's being; that is, an analytic subject that does not assert himself only by being different from the other. The revision of this topic undertaken throughout this study will reveal whether such an inclusion is possible or whether the confusion of tongues and the other as difference of the same are unwavering limits to psychoanalytic logic and practice. Both Levinas and Benjamin will be taken up in specific chapters, analysing in greater depth their relevance and importance concerning our proposed objectives.

CHAPTER THREE

A re-reading project

"It is true that experimental psychology is 'exact', but it can teach us little. Psycho-analysis is 'inexact', but it discloses unsuspected inter-relations and opens up layers of the mind hitherto inaccessible to research."

Ferenczi, "On the organization of the psycho-analytic movement", Second Nuremberg Congress, 1911 (1955, p. 301)

In the following chapters, the reader will set out on a journey of Ferenczi's work that does not pretend to be simply a thorough bibliographical incursion into different texts, attempting to do justice to them, but involves, rather, the production of new contents and meanings that, contained unspoken and hidden in the folds of the texts, are waiting to appear. As Héctor López (2007) correctly points out, "that is the work of the researcher: to allow the advent of a new meaning which is always produced by retroaction. The steps which enable that textual event to take place don't appear by 'inspiration' but in the course of hard work: by restoring the synchrony of the logical relationships in the diachronic dispersion of the texts under consideration" (p. 71).

We have insisted that Ferenczi's work has been systematically neglected and that the use of pejorative signifiers—referring to him as mad or

sick—has succeeded in obscuring not only his practice but also the validity of his theoretical and research production. But we will not spend time
complaining about this. On the contrary, we have been nourished by it,
put in a rather unusual place that relates to the need for absence as the
foundation of a particular discourse. As Michel Foucault (1984) indicates:
"In order for a return [return to] to take place, there must be forgetfulness,
not accidental forgetfulness, not the cover-up caused by some incom-
prehension, but essential and constitutive forgetfulness" (p. 17). In this
regard, Ferenczi, as an author, has to disappear so that the return to his
work can become possible. Readings of Ferenczi's work have, in general,
not been aware of that fundamental role that "being dead" plays in making room for the reading of authors' work. A direct manifestation of this is
the impossibility of separating Ferenczi the person—his historicity—from
the succession of events, experiences, and anecdotes that accumulate to
compose the narrative of an existence in time, and which appear chrono-
logically ordered in the various documents that make up the history of
psychoanalysis, although not that of the psychoanalytic movement.

The return to the Ferenczian oeuvre undertaken here intends to read
into the text that presence that has been omitted, bringing to light that
which has been forgotten about and that belongs to the very architecture
of the text, to its internal relationships, but which has not been revealed
in discourse. As Foucault (1984) points out, what appears in returns to
an author is not the creation of a new one (a researcher) regarding the
old text, but what is discovered in that new text "was there all along, it
was only a matter of reading it, everything is there, eyes had to be very
closed and ears very blocked not to have seen or heard it; and inversely,
it is not in this word or that, none of the visible and legible words says
what is now in question; this is about what is being said through the
words, in their space, in the distance that separates them" (p. 18). Therefore, by rediscovering the structural synchrony of the texts, invisible to
previous readings, we bring to the presence of what has not been read
in the text that which has always been waiting in the signifier folds but
which, at the same time, is not in any signifier but in the discursive
way in which those signifiers are, in the reading we propose, connected.
Thus, we can carry out the return to Ferenczi.

In the present study we also consider how psychoanalytical research
is not commensurate with the manner in which a scientific investigation
is carried out. This does not imply a deficiency on the part of the psychoanalytical method but, on the contrary, is one of its advantages, given

that psychoanalysis deals with that which science excludes and which, to put it bluntly, acquires only one name: the Real. Psychoanalytical logic, consistent with its own movement, functions with its own logic, following the Freudian procedure that led to the discovery of how the unconscious operates.

For this reason, we have commenced from a series of encounters. With respect to these, Freud has been discussed in relation to psychic trauma and war trauma. With Ferenczi, a dialogue has been established about trauma as an effect of the confusion of tongues, the reality of trauma, and the "confusion of tongues" as the name acquired by the real that challenges us in his work. With Walter Benjamin, translation has been addressed as a way of making language speak. To this end, the figure of the translator has been essential, operating as a way of either circumventing, or of "making with", the confusion of tongues, and the implications of this are significant in relation to the myth of the Tower of Babel. Developments with respect to the loss of the word on the part of First World War veterans (Benjamin, 1936) also play a part here. With Levinas, the figure of the other as other operates—the other as radically other and not as the other of me; the criticism of the thought of same-ness and of difference; and his attempts to make the other speak beyond the confusion of tongues. These contributions are of interest because they shed light on the issues introduced in the first part of this book and contribute to psychoanalytic therapy itself. Finally, we consider the concurrence with Lacan and his clinical work related to the real, his attempt to give an account of it without placing beforehand the representation or the image, as he tries to process the real through the real.

Ferenczi's writings from 1931 onwards have served to build and illustrate the concept of "confusion of tongues" in his oeuvre. As explained previously, this time period is being considered because it is here that the greatest theoretical distance between Freud and Ferenczi occurs. Moreover, these are the writings that earned Ferenczi his bad name within the analytic community, and caused the loss of credit in his work, which had been highly praised up to then. In the re-reading of these texts, an attempt has been made to insert a conceptual difference. Ferenczi's theoretical production between 1931 and his death in 1933 is not unconnected with the rest of his work and it is possible to trace links with and primary threads back to it. This illustrates the logic employed by Ferenczi in his theoretical and clinical work, loyal as he is to psychoanalytical presuppositions.

Thus it is possible to observe how a re-reading of Sándor Ferenczi's work allows us to understand some new consequences of the traumatic dimension of language that is worked out in his writings, permitting us, at the same time, to establish the importance and originality of his work in terms of the history of the psychoanalytic movement. We will discover how Ferenczi's elaborations from 1932 onwards are not a return to the Freudian theory of seduction but a new development around trauma, of great originality, and relevant to helping us address contemporary psychoanalysis. Furthermore, on this journey we will take up the notion of awakening, in order to find the place Sándor Ferenczi deserves in the history of the psychoanalytic movement.

This notion of awakening, developed by J.-A. Miller (1986), allows us to place Ferenczi within contemporary psychoanalysis. Awakening refers to the desire of an encounter with the real; nevertheless, such an encounter is not possible. Just as the awakening from the real is not possible, neither is it possible to awaken from the confusion of tongues. Awakening to the confusion of tongues makes reference to the production of a wish to awaken. For Miller, the analyst's wish has to do with the wish of awakening to the real. Ferenczi's technical innovations, even if initiated by a passion for the efficiency of analysis, can be read as attempts to produce a discomfort in the patient that dodges the dream of sense. The notion of awakening, construed from conceptualisations present in Miller's writings, has been used to place the relationships between the confusion of tongues and the real and the analyst's desire in Ferenczi's theoretical and clinical work.

In the following pages, the reader will find a re-reading of Sándor Ferenczi's oeuvre that rescues its importance for contemporary psychoanalysis, placing it within the logic of the psychoanalytic movement.

CHAPTER FOUR

Old ruptures, new connections

"Speech is telling the story of the trauma."
Sándor Ferenczi, *Clinical Diary*,
1 June 1932, (1932b, p. 113)

Sándor Ferenczi's oeuvre is extensive and prolific. Excluding his pre-analytic writings, his work, always produced with fervent psychoanalytic interest, maintains a permanent dialogue with, and a vindication of, the work of his teacher, Freud. Nevertheless, 1932 can be read as a turning point in his work, with the appearance of his paper "Confusion of tongues between adults and the child". This is the moment when his work achieved its greatest originality and also brought about his most significant rift with Freud. This paper, which constitutes a lecture Ferenczi read at the Wiesbaden Congress, was followed in the same year by his most fragmentary work, among which we highlight his *Clinical Diary* (1932b), "Notes and fragments" (1932c) and "Reflections on trauma" (1934), all published posthumously.

During his final years Ferenczi is concerned with questions regarding the etiology and cause of psychic trauma, the fragmentation of the psyche and the personality, and the role of trauma as real, as opposed to psychic, reality. The latter, together with the transferential and counter-transferential factors of his relationship with Freud, referred to in the correspondence of his final years, is the cause of greatest argument and estrangement between the two psychoanalysts. Ironically, despite the fragmentary character of Ferenczi's late writings, they consistently delve into the notions of fragmentation and of psychic trauma. Even though traces of this vital concern can be found in Ferenczi' previous clinical and theoretical work, his later writing will be taken up in depth; however, some earlier work will be taken into consideration insofar as it is relevant and reflects a coherent and logical derivation of these notions throughout his work. Freud, for his part, dedicates a great part of his writings to the topic of trauma, initially in relation to the etiology of hysteria and obsessive neurosis, and later on in relation to war neuroses (an issue that will be dealt with later), and, from 1920 onwards, with the phenomenon of traumatic dreams and repetition.

Giorgio Agamben's book *Remnants of Auschwitz: The Witness and the Archive* (1999) allows us to explore a different dimension of war trauma; not the one that psychoanalysts, neurologists, and psychiatrists were discussing at the beginning of the twentieth century, namely that of the First World War, but that of the military conflict and its horrors that can be foreseen in Freud's writing: the Second World War. From the writings of Primo Levi, and other survivors of concentration camps, Agamben rescues the figure of the *Muslim* as that prisoner who has lost all human attributes, including, of course, the power of speech. Thus, for Agamben, what is not said is not what is excluded from the said, but rather what mobilises and underpins that which is said. The *Muslim*—in the conceptual construction elaborated by Agamben—makes evident the loss of the subject's possibility of emergence and, by his condition in relationship to language, his inability to provide testimony of his experience. In this way, the Muslim suggests a frontier with the real inasmuch as he makes evident what the subject cannot testify, not as the subject's other but as his permanent possibility and condition in the process of subjectivation and de-subjectivation.

Levinas suggests a way of disposing thought that paves the way to the other being able to accept philosophy's presence without becoming its object. The Levinasian labyrinth consists in how to think that *other* of thought without reducing it to a concept, bearing in mind the fact that thought operates by making *a* sameness of the *other*, that is, that object of thought. Thus, hand in hand with the traced lines of thought, Levinas tries to give testimony to that which cannot be testified: even though the other *other* is the structural lost of all thought, it is precisely because it is missing and because it pierces that which exists and which insists in the production of thoughts that, even though they do not manage to produce more than samenesses, they still attempt to skirt the frontier of that aspect of the real that cannot be enclosed.

Walter Benjamin is another Jewish author who analyses in detail the possibilities of language in order to wipe out that impossibility of signifying that dwells in the word. Re-reading his Jewish tradition, so interwoven with the verbal origin of the world, he inserts the reflection of language in the topic of translation and, in particular, in the latter's structural impossibility. The mythical ancestry of common languages having been lost, the confusion of tongues is the real that dwells in all language: a hole of the impossibility of signifying that is, nevertheless, the motor of all idiomatic production. Thus, rather than aiming at a metalanguage, human wealth lives in an *intermediate language* that presents the confusion of tongues to the world.

This other way of addressing thought and language, forcing thought to stand apart from any attempts to inscribe its object within philosophical metaphysics, goes hand in hand with what Jorge Alemán refers to as *antiphilosophy*, a term borrowed from a lecture by Lacan. At the extremes of the technical tools that promise an idyll of the limitless, outside the mediation of castration, antiphilosophical thought—that threshold between philosophy and psychoanalysis—aims at listening to that which epochs—time taken by humanity to signify trauma—do not assimilate, the remnant detached from its temporality and its significance, none other than its *real*. What designates the vectors of movement of psychoanalysis itself is, precisely, the real; not the psychoanalyst's will. Psychoanalysis appears as it monitors and listens along that path. Following that silence and daring to think differently, Ferenczi arrives at the thought of the confusion of tongues as the real that speaks of the structural lost of all significance, which in turn serves as motor to the symbolic.

CHAPTER FIVE

The history of "Confusion of tongues between adults and the child"

> "I should not be surprised if this paper, like some others which I have published of late years, gave you the impression of a certain *naivete in* my outlook. It may strike you as odd that anyone, after working at analysis for twenty-five years, should suddenly begin to regard with wonder the fact of psychic traumas. It is like an engine-driver I knew, who when pensioned off after fifty years' service, used to go down to the station every afternoon and gaze in wonder at a train just going out, often exclaiming: 'Isn't a locomotive a marvelous invention!'"
>
> Child-analysis in the analysis of adults
> (Ferenczi, 1931, p. 142)

Ferenczi's article "Confusion of tongues between adults and the child. (The language of tenderness and of passion" (1932a) was the opening presentation of the twelfth Congress of Psychoanalysis in Wiesbaden, Germany, held on 12 September 1932. Ferenczi presented his paper to various psychoanalysts of that time, but Freud did not attend due to health problems. Even though Freud did not listen to the lecture, he was familiar with it, since Ferenczi had read it to him at his home some time before. Freud's response was decisive: he immediately rejected it. Among the analysts who did listen to it were: "Anna Freud, Federn, Alexander, Jekels, Jones, de Groot, Brunswick, Simmel, Harnick, Bonaparte, Sterba, Reck, Balint, Deutsch, Rado, Weiss, Odrir, Glover, Roheim, Menninger, de Sausseiere [Saussure]" (Masson, 1984, p. 15). The rejection of the lecture was widespread: the new methods presented, the resonance of a return to the theory of seduction, the focus on child sexual abuse, the emphasis on the work dealing with difficult cases, and the evident rupture with Freud's thought were the main causes attributed to the uneasiness that it produced. Nevertheless, this is not the start of the Freud-Ferenczi conflict, which can probably be traced as far back as the publication in 1924 of the joint paper by Ferenczi and Rank entitled "The development of psychoanalysis" (1924).

On the other hand, it is strange that this paper in particular should have generated such a stir because, even if it marks a turning point in Ferenczi's oeuvre, it is not inconsistent with what he had been producing up to then. Since his pre-analytic writings, Ferenczi had expressed his interest in difficult cases, and he had presented unorthodox ideas about psychiatry and technical innovations for the treatment of his patients. All of this was before the start of his relationship with Freud (see, for example, Ferenczi, 1902).

What is generally emphasised when Freud's rejection with respect to Ferenczi's work is taken up, is the topic of the return to the first Freudian *neurotica*. The abandonment of the seduction theory on Freud's part has been the target of many hypotheses. For Jones (1953), it seemed to be a breakthrough in psychoanalytic theory, a result of the auto-analysis undertaken by Freud himself (pp. 265–266); others, like Anzieu (1975, pp. 311–315), Max Schur (1972, pp. 113–114), and Sulloway (1979, p. 205) have agreed with the abandonment of the *neurotica* and have taken it as a guideline for their own work; for others, like Masson (1984), on the contrary, abandonment is interpreted as a loss of courage on the part of Freud; and Krull (1979), going even further, also sees the abandonment of the seduction theory as a step backwards, attributing it to Freud's ambivalence with respect to his own father (referred to by Rachman, 1989, p. 184). These latter comments reflect the voice of a tradition in psychoanalysis that has always kept alive the importance of the first Freudian neurotic. In this regard, Ferenczi continues to be taken up by these authors because it was he who opened the door to the thought of emotional abuse as trauma.

It is not clear if for Freud this was, in fact, such a ludicrous statement, since he continued to bring it up in his writings and lectures subsequent to the supposed abandonment of the seduction theory. In his twenty-third lecture from *Introductory Lectures on Psycho-Analysis* (1917), entitled "The paths to the formation of symptoms", Freud states: "Phantasies of being seduced are of particular interest, because so often they are not phantasies but real memories" (p. 370). With ease, Ferenczi's commentators affirm that Freud abandoned his theory of traumatic seduction before 1900, but Freud's later references to the same are, at any rate, omitted. The most decisive one can be found in "From the history of an infantile neurosis" (1918b). There Freud writes:

> When once the Grusha scene had been assimilated—the first experience that he could really remember, and one which he had remembered without any conjectures or intervention on my part—the problem of the treatment had every appearance of having been solved. From that time forward there were no more resistances; all that remained to be done was to collect and to co-ordinate. The old trauma theory of the neuroses, which was after all built up upon impressions gained from psycho-analytic practice, had suddenly come to the front once more. (p. 94)

According to Sabourin (1984), at times, Freud seems to leave out any new reference to the old traumatic theory (as in the case study of Schreber) and, at others, he seems to come back to it, as, "for example, in 1924 when he confirms that 'seduction has preserved a certain etiological importance, and even today I consider valid certain developments presented here ...'" (p. 17). Sabourin is referring to a footnote that Freud includes in 1924 to his 1896 text "Further remarks on the neuro-psychoses of defence" (1896b). In that article, Freud treats seduction as a concrete act and not as a fantasy or masquerade. The footnote added in 1924 says:

> This section is dominated by an error which I have since repeatedly acknowledged and corrected. At that time I was not yet able to distinguish between my patients' phantasies about their childhood years and their real recollections. As a result, I attributed to the aetiological factor of seduction a significance and universality which it does not possess. When this error had been overcome, it became possible to obtain an insight into the spontaneous manifestations of

the sexuality of children which I described in my *Three Essays on the Theory of Sexuality* (1905d). Nevertheless, we need not reject everything written in the text above. Seduction retains a certain aetiological importance, and even to-day I think some of these psychological comments are to the point. (p. 168)

Other examples could be mentioned in Freud, such as the real fact of the death of the father in *Totem and Taboo* (1912–13) and the real identity and later assassination of Moses the Man in *Moses and Monotheism* (1939a). Thus, it can be observed that Freud did not assume a definite stance with respect to the seduction theory. This is supported by the fact that "in some letters to Fliess, censored by Freud's official descendants, Max Schur has found details which help us to understand the magnitude of Freud's conflict in this respect. Unlike his successors, Freud never leaned towards definite opinions in favour or against the seduction theory" (Sabourin, 1984, p. 15.).

Sabourin (1984) clarifies a point which helps in understanding a characteristic feature of the German language with respect to seduction. In German, the word that both Freud and Fliess use to refer to seduction is *Verführung*, which has an active meaning; that is, seduction is used as "disorientation, deviation, in this case deviation of the child's desire by the adult, and not seduction taken in the passive sense, as it occurs in French, namely, seduction as charm or attribute of the person who tries to be someone else's object of desire, nor seduction as fantasy (original or not), and even less 'seduction as destiny'" (Baudrillard, 1979, cited by Sabourin, 1984, p. 15).

Ferenczi was conscious of reviving the old controversy about trauma and, to this end, suggested rather intimate motives, in relation to his illness. In a letter dated 20 July 1930, he writes to Freud:

"Though somewhat sooner than you, Professor, I too am preoccupied with the problem of death, naturally in regard to my own destiny and prospects for the future. Part of my love for the corporeal Me appears to have sublimated itself in scientific interests, and this subjective factor has made me sensitive, I think, to the psychic and other processes that take place in neurotics in moments of mortal danger, real or presumed. That was the path which led me to revive the theory of traumatism, apparently obsolete (or at least temporarily pushed aside)." (Quoted by Dupont, 1995 p. xiv)

Even if the presence of this argument becomes evident with respect to the reality of trauma, we observe that, for Freud, the outdated traumatic theory had far from expired. This leads us necessarily to suppose the presence of a "something else" in Ferenczi's writing of 1932, which added fuel to the fire of the Freudian belligerence. And indeed there is an aspect that has been less attended to in the Freud-Ferenczi controversy regarding the *confusion of tongues* related to the drive factor, which could be expressed as follows: while Freud thought that within each subject there is a deadly element, for Ferenczi that deadly element appears as a result of the other; it is caused by the traumatic effect of the other's action; if this was not so, there would be no reason for it to erupt (Gutiérrez-Peláez, 2009). Nevertheless, Freud's comings and goings can also be found regarding this particular issue. According to what he writes in the conclusion to *Three Essays on the Theory of Sexuality* (1905), "the external influences of seduction are capable of provoking interruptions of the latency period or even its cessation, and that in this connection the sexual instinct of children proves in fact to be polymorphously perverse" (p. 234). External traumatic factors, such as seductions of children by adults, can have catastrophic effects on libidinal development, either by hampering it, retarding it, or diverting it.

In a footnote in *The Ego and the Id* (1923b), Freud affirms the following:

> The battle with the obstacle of an unconscious sense of guilt is not made easy for the analyst. Nothing can be done against it directly, and nothing indirectly but the slow procedure of unmasking its unconscious repressed roots, and of thus gradually changing it into a *conscious* sense of guilt. [...] it must be honestly confessed that here we have another limitation to the effectiveness of analysis; after all, analysis does not set out to make pathological reactions impossible, but to give the patient's ego *freedom* to decide one way or the other. (p. 50, italics in original)

Here Freud comes up against a barrier for psychoanalysis, an issue beyond which it is impossible to go forward. The unconscious sense of guilt is a deadly element of the death drive, impossible to disentangle through psychoanalysis.

Events seem to prove that Freud played an active role in preventing the publication in English of Ferenczi's paper, which had been presented at the Congress of Wiesbaden. Rachman (1989) presents a series of evidence that proves that Freud, helped by other members of the analytic community, deliberately excluded Ferenczi's article from all later publications. Rachman's evidence is based on comments made by Jeffrey Masson about Freud's unpublished correspondence during the time he was secretary of Freud's archives. Anna Freud gave Masson access to the material before the construction of the Freud Museum was undertaken. According to Masson (1984, p. 145), he found the material by accident in a desk drawer at Freud's house in Maresfield Gardens. It consisted of a series of letters whose existence even Anna seemed to have ignored. Another of Rachman's sources confirms the material translated into French by the Le Coq-Héron group. In a letter quoted by Sylwan (1984, p. 108), Freud warns Eitington on 29 August 1932, that either Ferenczi will read a different work to the "Confusion of tongues ..." or he will not read anything at all. For Freud, the work was "unreachable" and caused an unpleasant impression. This bad impression on Freud's part regarding the article caused Ferenczi great pain.

Sometime later, Ernest Jones himself will play a key role in excluding, once and for all, Ferenczi's article. Just like Freud, Eitington, and other analysts of the first generation, Jones rejected the content of the work on "confusion of tongues". His omission appears as a strategic move that starts with his refusal to translate Ferenczi's paper. During the thirties, many analysts resorted to English versions of articles to be up-to-date with the advances of psychoanalysis. For this reason, the papers presented at Congresses used to be quickly translated into English for publication, but Ferenczi's lecture did not have that luck, despite his wish to have it translated, although it was, indeed, read at the Congress. According to Rachman's evidence, Jones lied to Ferenczi, telling him that his article would appear translated in the *International Journal of Psycho-Analysis* (Masson, 1984, p. 151). Ferenczi himself wrote to Jones on 22 March 1933, thanking him for wanting to publish his paper for the Congress in the English magazine (unpublished letter written in English, kept in the London Jones archives, discovered by Masson, 1984, pp. 151–152.) Finally, Jones translated the article but he lied to Ferenczi, telling him that he would publish it. Later on, after Ferenczi's death in May 1933, Jones spoke openly about his feelings and impressions regarding Ferenczi's article. The following letter, addressed to Freud during that same month, which has been neither published nor translated, was retrieved by Masson from the Jones archives in England, is quoted in its entirety:

> "It is about Ferenczi's Congress paper that I am now writing. Eitingon did not wish to allow it to be read at the Congress, but I persuaded him. I thought at the time of asking you about its publication in the *Zeitscrift*. I felt he would be offended if it were not translated into English and so asked his permission for this. He seemed gratified, and we have not only translated it but set it up in type as the first chapter in the July number. Since his death, I have been thinking over the removal of the personal reasons for publishing it. Others also have suggested that it now be withdrawn and I quote the following passage from a letter of Mrs. Riviere's with which I agree: 'Now that Ferenczi has died, I wondered whether you will not reconsider publishing his last paper. It seems to me it can only be damaging to him and a discredit, while now that he is no longer to be hurt by its not being published, no good purpose could be served by it. Its scientific contentions and its statements about analytic practice are just a tissue of delusions, which can only discredit psychoanalysis and give credit to its opponents. It cannot be supposed that all *Journal* readers will appreciate the mental condition of the writer, and in this respect one has to think of posterity, too!' I therefore think it best to withdraw the paper unless I hear from you that you have any wish to the contrary." (Unpublished letter, Jones Archives, London, cited in Masson, p. 152. & Rachman, 1989, p. 199)

Thus the destiny of the article's publication remained in Freud's hands. Rachman (1989) affirms that there is no evidence of Freud's answer. Nevertheless, there is a reference regarding this issue in a letter that Jones sends to Brill on 20 June 1933, where he writes that, in order to please Ferenczi, he had printed the article for the July edition of the *Zeitcrift* but, after consulting with Freud, decided not to publish it. Brill, in turn, answered that he agreed with him, stating that the less the article was mentioned, the better. What happened to Jones' translation of the paper is not known. It will not be until 1949, sixteen years later, that the article is definitively published in English, translated by Balint, Ferenczi's loyal and devout pupil. That translation, however, presents some difficulties, especially because Balint translated two different words (*Zunge* and *Sprache*) as if they were the same word, always writing *tongue* in their place, which in our view has been one of the causes of the erroneous reading of the article (Gutiérrez-Peláez, 2006, 2010).

Even more curious than its exclusion in English is the fact that the article was prevented from being published in Hungarian magazines on psychology, especially when we consider that Hungary was Ferenczi's native land. In an article by Hidas (1993; quoted by Rachman, 1997b, p. 476), who was the first president of the Ferenczi Society in Hungary, we note that the work was published only once and for the first time in 1971; that is, thirty-nine years after the Congress of Wiesbaden, in a book by Béla Buda entitled *Psychoanalysis and its Modern Tendencies*, in remembrance of Ferenczi's oeuvre. After that publication, the work is once again forgotten and Hidas affirms that it is not taken up by contemporary Hungarian psychoanalysis.

After the publication of the article in English, many psychoanalysts supported the work, among them Eric Fromm, who affirmed: "As anybody who reads it can convince himself, it is a paper of extraordinary profundity and brilliance—one of the most valuable papers in the whole psychoanalytic literature; it contains, however, certain important though subtle deviations from Freud's thought" (Fromm, 1959, n. 3, p. 165, quoted by Rachman, 1989, p. 200). Many other analysts have expressed their admiration for the article. Nevertheless, we have not found any author who has highlighted the concept of "confusion of tongues" as is our intention in the present study. In an article published in 1989 in the *Journal of American Academy of Psychoanalysis* (1989, pp. 181–205) entitled "Confusion of tongues: The Ferenczian metaphor for childhood seduction and emotional trauma", Arthur W. M. Rachman aims at elucidating a fundamental element in the "confusion of tongues" that initially seemed to be in accordance with our notion of its status as metaphor, and, as such, its place in the production of language.

Rachman (1989) suggests four possible readings of this metaphor: 1) the child who resorts to the adult in search of tenderness is sexually abused by the adult who is looking for passion; thus, the child confuses tenderness with passion; 2) a patient abused when he was a child relives the aggression experienced in childhood with the person of the analyst in transference when the latter maintains an insensitive, distant attitude and is emotionally cold; as a result of this behaviour, the analyst confuses the analysand once again; 3) a level of confusion of tongues takes place between Freud and Ferenczi, produced by the article itself; 4) a confusion of tongues between Ferenczi and the analytical community occurs, triggered, in Rachman's words, by an oedipal conflict between Ferenczi and Jones for the love of Freud the father, which gained the status of trauma for Ferenczi. It is possible to see how Ferenczi's readers and commentators, just when they seem to unveil an essential knowledge about his work, conceal it again. Some of the most persistent veils thrown over Ferenczi's work, in order to hide it, are: reference to it as psychopathological; the ascription to him psychoanalytical symptoms, either of neurosis or psychosis; and the claim that these are what drives his later work.

Other authors proceed in the same manner: Blum (1994) considers that "Confusion of tongues between adults and the child" is the article of a dying analysand in a state of regression to his analyst with whom he finds himself identified (p. 872), thus dismissing Ferenczi's last work as a production of illness, a theoretical posture criticised by Berman (1995). (With what ease a certain tendency of psychoanalysis uses a kind of pseudo-analysis applied to the first generation of analysts, disregarding a fundamental factor: that they are signifiers and not persons. How could they otherwise be read and communicate something?) Just as Nietzsche used to say that Kant freed the beast only to put it back in its cage (he acknowledged phenomenological perception, postulating at the same time *the thing-in-itself*), we can say that Rachman gets close to an awakening when he refers to the "confusion of tongues" as metaphor, but he puts the wealth of his discovery back to sleep when he sets out to develop what he understands by metaphor. We also observe that Rachman continues to highlight the innocent vision of childhood.

This is a paradoxical, and recurrent, aspect of analysts and authors who write about Ferenczi (Blum, 1994; Jacobson, 1994; Press, 2006; Rachman, 1989; Zaslow, 1998, among others); these authors read his work, emphasise his brilliant mind, and affirm that one of his great achievements was to realise that adults impose their ideas upon the child's behaviour, erasing in this way their reality. In such readings, however, these authors act in the same way with regard to Ferenczi: they impose their own ideas, silencing that which is most interesting and profound in the Hungarian psychoanalyst's work. The dimension that they rescue is a very basic one and not particularly original with respect to the "confusion of tongues". In addition, it is a basic psychological assertion and not a psychoanalytical one. Nevertheless, authors such as Modell (1991) have managed to give regard to the "confusion of tongues" beyond sexual abuse. In the latter's case, for example, he places the "confusion of tongues" at a level that occurs in the construction of the child's reality: the "confusion of tongues" is the conflict between the construction of reality of the child and the adult's reality (p. 228), resulting in a conflict of desires and needs. Harris and Aron (1997), on their part, brilliantly attempt to rescue a semiotic theory from Ferenczi. These formulations are fundamental to an understanding of Ferenczi's oeuvre and his thinking, and we wish to start out from them in order to take the concept of "confusion of tongues" one step further.

The merit of Rachman's journey has to do with having withdrawn the dimension of the "confusion of tongues" from its purely imaginary status. In this way, two different dimensions are sketched out, upon which "the confusion of tongues" may be read: an imaginary dimension, in the relationship between the innocent child and the passionate adult who abuses him; and a symbolic dimension, in which the "confusion of tongues" operates as metaphor. But it would seem that the Ferenczian discovery aims at a "beyond" of this symbolic dimension of the confusion of tongues; namely, as an opening of its real dimension. A new reading of "Confusion of tongues between adults and the child" (1932a) becomes necessary; one that will permit us to listen to the hoarser sounds of his words, allowing that real dimension to appear and to acquire presence.

On translation and the confusion of tongues: a "beyond" for the confusion of tongues

"The correct way for freeing oneself from it: demechanization and dehypnotizing."

Sándor Ferenczi, *Clinical Diary*,
17 March 1932 (1932a, p. 63)

Ferenczi's 1932 article, "Confusion of tongues between adults and the child. (The language of tenderness and of passion)" (1932a), permits the reading of a subtext that runs through it from beginning to end, which can be drawn out precisely from its title: "confusion of tongues". This subtext gains importance insofar as it puts us at the centre of the issue of translation, referring us necessarily to the biblical myth of the tower of Babel, place of origin of the confusion of tongues. The myth of the tower of Babel will be thought about according to a structural logic consistent with the ways in which myths are read from the perspective of psychoanalytical doctrine. Myth, in turn, is always connected with the opening to the real, when the confines of the symbolic define its shoreline. As Lacan points out in "Transference", Book VIII of his Seminars (1961):

… when one comes […] to a certain term of what can be obtained on the plane of episteme, of knowledge, in order to go beyond (we can

43

easily conceive that there is a limit in so far as on the plane of knowledge there is only what is accessible to the pure and simple operation
of the law of the signifier). In the absence of well-advanced experimental conquests, it is clear that in many domains—and in domains
which we for our part can pass over—there will be a pressure to let
myth speak. […] We see […] myths emerging, when they are required,
to supply for the gap in what cannot be assured dialectically. (p. 143)

In this way, it is possible to draw out the significance of the myth of the
tower of Babel in order to think about the Ferenczian proposal around
the "confusion of tongues" with respect to translation. To begin with, it
is possible to affirm, according to the journey suggested by Derrida in
"Des Tours de Babel" (1979), that in Hebrew the word Babel is homophonic with another: "confusion". Thus it follows, in the structural
logic of myth, that Babel, which is Confusion, produces the confusion of
tongues. To be able to draw out the wealth of nuances that appear from
undertaking this reading of Ferenczi's article, we consider it essential
to use as a tool Derrida's article about the confusion of tongues, one of
the most valuable writings regarding the way in which the myth of the
tower of Babel sheds light on the issue of translation.

Derrida's article appears, in the first instance, as a challenge for
its translators, since it involves translating a text about translation.
Translation itself takes us to the core of the problem: namely, is translation possible? And, if it is, in what way is it so, since the babelisation
has produced the confusion of tongues? Translators of Derrida's text
say, wanting Derrida to speak on their behalf: "One should never pass
over in silence the question of the tongue in which the question of the
tongue is raised and into which a discourse on translation is translated."
(Derrida, 1979, p. 166). The destruction of the tower and of the project
of a universal language (if they do correspond to two different archi-
tectures) requires the need for translation, making it impossible at the
same time; a sort of necessary impossibility. Translation turns into con-
demnation, which can only lead to frustration, since there would seem
to be an unavoidable dimension to the confusion of tongues. Derrida's
translators know it, and so does he, who does not ignore the fact that
his writing is, at the same time, translation, and not only because in
it he translates a text by Benjamin regarding translation (text which
in turn has been translated by someone else). It is with Derrida's aid
that we will be able to introduce Benjamin's thought, which will be just

as valuable in extracting the importance of the concept "confusion of tongues", conceived from the point of view of psychoanalysis.

Derrida works on the problem of translation starting from the myth of Babel. He points out in his writing that the "... proper name of God [YHWH], come from God ... is divided enough in the tongue, already, to signify, also, confusedly, 'confusion'" (Derrida, 1979, p. 170.) Derrida is interested in this homophonic question of the connection between Babel and Confusion because he highlights the fact that confusion is the material itself in which the tower of language is constructed. Language is necessarily confusion and speech, babelisation. In this way, when myth refers to the previous state of the construction of the tower, where language has not yet been confused, Derrida is making reference to that immaculate place that we have already indicated in Ferenczi: a place where men are still innocent children, uncontaminated by desire and not pierced by language. The fact that the tower is always the *ruin* of the tower is understood, just as language is always a cut, and its acquisition implies a significant loss. The whole subject of translation aims at operations that are made starting from that incision established by language, in the transactions that flow through a blank, empty space and which never consolidate themselves in a metalanguage. The mad relationship with language, whether taken from mystical writings (Sor Juana Inés de la Cruz or Saint Francis of Assisi) or from psychosis (Schreber's *Grundsprache*), proves that something of that cut and that loss has not managed to fully consolidate; there is still something missing, that structuring lack that we have here called babelisation or confusion (of tongues).

It is amazing that no critic of, or commentator on, Ferenczi has highlighted the Babel-like resonances suggested both in the title and in the content of the 1932 article. Ferenczi describes a dimension of the confusion: the tender language of the child is confused with the passionate language of the adult. There is a confusion of tongues in the sense that the tender emotions of the child are read as passionate by the adult, who reacts on the basis of his own sexual dispositions, which are totally different from those to which the child has access, due to his condition as infant. The child, overcome by fear, subjects himself and identifies with the aggressor. This generates a clear split in his psyche (see Gutiérrez-Peláez, 2010), becoming both aggressor and aggressed, and feeling irreconcilable guilt and pain. A psychic split has operated in him in order to preserve his psychic functioning; such is the paradox Ferenczi presents.

But there is another dimension of that confusion of tongues in this article; Balint, a disciple and translator of Ferenczi's work into English, falls into it this time: he merges the *Sprache* and the *Zunge* in one sole signifier: *tongue*. He seems unable to escape from the English translation of the Bible where the homologation is present and from which Ferenczi is spared in his article, employing both *Zunge* and *Sprache*. Spanish is freed from this confusion, from which English is not exempt: in Spanish, *lengua* is at the same time organ of speech (anatomic) and language. In other languages, like Hebrew, it is not the tongue that speaks, but the lip.

Translation is an issue that has always been present in psychoanalytic thinking. Freud (1940) suggested:

> it is evident that everything new that we have inferred must nevertheless be translated back into the language of our perceptions, from which it is simply impossible for us to free ourselves. [...] And if, for instance, we say: "At this point an unconscious memory intervened", what that means is: "At this point something occurred of which we are totally unable to form a conception, but which, if it had entered our consciousness, could only have been described in such and such a way." (pp. 196–197)

In the myth of Babel, translation is also transmutation of materials: "... brick becoming stone and tar serving as mortar." (Derrida, 1979, p. 168). The psychoanalyst confronts in his practice and in his thought, the problems of translation: that the language of his patient will not confuse itself with his own. He also confronts the issue suggested by Derrida regarding how to translate a written text in various languages, since that which the patient brings to his sessions as discourse, wishing to substantiate his own word, is usually a polyphony of voices that speak through his mouth. This is because the problem of hypnosis is undoubtedly a key topic of psychoanalysis, far from having been left outside its sphere because Freud chose to discard it as a therapeutic method. If there is one thing that serves as proof of the routine of clinical work, it is that hypnosis is a key factor, but in quite a different manner to that of Breuer and Janet as well as the initial (pre-psychoanalytical) Freud. Undoubtedly Ferenczi (1932b), when he refers to the "the correct way for freeing oneself from it: demechanization and dehypnotizing" (p. 63), was the one who most realised the validity of hypnosis, in as much as patients arrive hypnotised at the sessions, taking as their own the words of others, which, like orders, dictate their destinies.

Even before 1906—a prolific year for Ferenczi during which he made important contributions to the study of hypnotic therapy, his technique, and counter-indications, and a time when he started to concern himself also about the laws that regulated hypnotic therapy in his country—the Hungarian psychoanalyst began to make a turn that, more than a movement against, seems to be a movement towards the same Möbius strip that reveals the step from hypnotising to dehypnotising. The main characteristic of hypnosis has to do with the effect of the word on the person, who acts out someone else's orders as if they were his own, leaving no trace of the hypnotist who, like a puppeteer of the word, appropriates the will delegated by the hypnotised subject. The role of hypnosis shifts, since how could patients be subjected to it? They already carry sufficient words to make them produce new ones.

But is the destiny of the confusion of tongues necessarily hypnosis or is it, on the contrary, the clinical tool that the psychoanalyst has at his disposal to produce an awakening to that real that is the confusion of tongues? If we have placed Ferenczi on the side of awakening, his method would seem to go in the opposite direction to that lulling sleep produced by the hypnotic trance.

As López points out (1990),

> if the psychoanalytical movement can be summed up as a kind of opposition between sleep and awakening, we should place Ferenczi completely on the side of awakening; and by this I mean to an encounter with something unknown, lying in the order of the real, if you like, and which is not something natural to the subject; what is natural is a tendency to sleep, to assimilation, to what is already known; and awakening is an anti-natural function. Analysis or, should I say, the analyst's wish, tends to produce an awakening. (Without page. See also López, 2010)

Ferenczi becomes aware of that sleepiness and can also read it as a symptom of the analytical practice of his time. He therefore sets out to decipher ways of carrying that regressive tendency towards sleep in the opposite direction, boosting an awakening to the real. He knows, above all, that the patient arrives hypnotised, asleep, in the profound sleep of that palimpsest that speaks within him. Thus, each session of analysis operates like a scene with very special features, where the characters and voices that enter the scene through the voice of the patient are numerous. The patient names as his own a series of voices belonging previously to other bodies, which have been forging their disguise of superego. Hidden between the characters he narrates and the words he pronounces, the voices and places of enunciation of the superego are drawn. Those places are not established for life, but rotate, transform, and metamorphose, each session having its own characteristics. Changes of place can occur during the same session. In this way, through the analyst's work, the analysand starts to realise that those voices, phrases, words, etc., enounced as his own, belong in fact to other characters who have lodged in his unconscious like a cruel, superegoic plan.

In the polyphony of voices of others that the patient brings, unaware, in his hypnotic trance, of the alienation of those words, he forces the psychoanalyst to a slow and cautious labour of surgery and frameworking, facilitating the patient's awakening and giving back the word to those who initially pronounced it and which the patient has incorporated as law. The much criticised *Küsstechnik*, or Ferenczian "kissing technique", could be re-read in this regard: the kiss as metaphor of that place where tongues converge—or the lips, if we adhere to the literal meaning of the Hebrew translation—which in this context could be understood as the correct manner of dealing with translation.

> Let us accompany this movement of love, the gesture of this loving one (*liebend*) that is at work in the translation. It does not reproduce, does not restitute, does not represent; as to the essential, it does not *render* the meaning of the original except at that point of contact or caress, the infinitely small of meaning. It extends the body of languages, it puts languages into symbolic expansion, and symbolic here means that, however little restitution is to be accomplished, the larger, the new vaster aggregate, has still to *reconstitute* something. (Derrida, 1979, p. 190, italics in original)

Thus, when Freud is horrified at the words of Ferenczi's patient, who repeats in social circles: "I am allowed to *kiss Papa Ferenczi*, as often as I like" (1932, p. 2; quoted by Stanton, 1997, p. 49), we could say that Freud (in his own translation) did not read those words between the lines, or at least not beyond the details of the love of transference. This contains a metaphor that deserves to be re-read. In a reinterpretation of the words with which the patient boasted of an imaginary amorous relationship with Ferenczi, it is possible to read, in this context, that in her analysis a level of understanding of the lips existed, precisely because through Ferenczi's mouth she could hear the echo of her own desire and not its denial by his words, which would not go beyond the repetition of the situation that trauma established. If we consider the literal meaning of the Hebrew translation, where language is termed "lip", and if the kiss is understood as a dimension of love, of its operability, it can be seen that in the opening of the lip disposed to the kiss, the dimension of the *béance*, the gap exempt and untouched in translation, is revealed, which, paradoxically, is the very motor of translation.[1]

Ferenczi knows this clearly. He says that "speech is telling the story of the trauma" (1932b, p. 113) and in that regard he articulates trauma as trauma of language. Ferenczi knows the role and the value of love in the union of the parts. He knows that "[w]ithout sympathy: there is no healing" (1932b, p. 200). As an expert analyst in difficult cases, he is confronted in his everyday clinical practice with the *shapelessness* of the split mind, which takes the form of a "broken amphora", to use Benjamin's metaphor quoted by Derrida:

> "For, just as the fragments of the amphora, if one is to be able to reconstitute the whole, must be contiguous in the smallest details, but not identical to each other, so instead of rendering itself similar to the meaning of the original, the translation should rather, in a movement of love and in full detail, pass into its own language the mode of intention of the original: thus, just as the debris become recognizable as fragments of the same amphora, original and translations become recognizable as fragments of a larger language."
> (Derrida, 1979, pp. 189–190)

That larger language, in the case of psychoanalysis, has to do with one's own desire, with grasping something of that correspondence that exists between the words themselves and the authenticity of that desire expressed through them. As J.-A. Miller (1986) also points out, "the analyst's desire is the desire of awakening" (p. 120). Here the desire of the analyst and the love of the translator play their part; in this context they have merged until they have become the same thing, the union of the parts, the voices, the places of enunciation of the words that inhabit discourse, making them enter into the ways of being of language itself.

The dimension of love has been re-signified in analysis, beyond the love of transference, which could only understand the *Küsstechnik* dimension as an encounter of erogenous zones (skin, pores, and flesh) and not of *tongues*. "Let us not forget that Babel names a struggle for the sur-vival [sic] of the name, the tongue or the lips" (Derrida, 1979, p. 183).

But is the totality of the elements of the tower of Babel myth exhausted at this point, or are there new seams in it that will allow us to reflect on the Ferenczian "confusion of tongues"? It is important at this point, therefore, to set out on a journey through the tower of Babel myth that can offer us important variables to contribute to the issue of the confusion of tongues, placing it in relation to its biblical origin.

CHAPTER SEVEN

Babel and the tower of Babel

And they said, "Go to, let us build us a city and a tower, whose top may reach unto heaven; and let us make us a name, lest we be scattered abroad upon the face of the whole earth."

Genesis 11: 4

What do we know of the tower of Babel? According to the Bible (Genesis 10: 1–32 and 11: 1–9), Noah begot Shem, who in turn begot Cush, who begot Nimrod, first powerful man on earth. The latter ordered the construction of the tower of Babel, a tower of immense magnitude that reached the heavens. Some famous images have depicted with creative and fantastic imagination what the tower might have been like: two paintings by Bruegel the Elder, an image by Monsù Desiderio, one by Frans Francken the Younger, and a twelfth century ivory plaque in Salerno Cathedral, just to name a few.

It can be said that even when various representations of it have been preserved, dispersed in Europe since the High Middle Ages (in the capitals of the Doge's Palace and the Monreale cathedral, in the window of Saint Martin of Colmar, in the murals of Saint Savin sur-Gartempe, in the Pisa cemetery, work by Benozzo Gozzoli),

> there exists a certain geographical position of its image in space
> and time: in Germany, the Netherlands and Flanders at the time its
> peoples attempted to secede from Rome. (Benet, 1990, p. 17)

Other examples are: the earliest extant example of a painting on the
theme in the Maurithuis in The Hague; those by Bril and von Kaulbach
in the Dahlem at Berlin; by van Cleef in Prague; van Troyen in Dresden;
and by Jan van Scorel in Venice. It seems that there are no known representations of the tower of Babel until the Cotton Bible of the fifth and
sixth centuries, but with Bruegel the Elder that the tower gains prominence in painting. Between 1550 and 1650 numerous altarpieces make
reference to the tower.

However, we are not interested in these works as artistic creations, or
in relation to their aesthetic merit—which is undoubtedly superb—but
insofar as they constitute translations in themselves.[1] But, is it possible,
from this multiplicity of representations, to rebuild the whole tower?
Is the sum of translations, be they pictorial, lyric, or semantic, whether
forms or images, sufficient to reconstruct the *Urbild* of Babel?

According to the American writer Paul Auster (1985):

> As for the Tower itself, legend had it that one third of the struc-
> ture sank into the ground, one third was destroyed by fire, and one
> third was left standing. God attacked it in two ways in order to
> convince man that the destruction was a divine punishment and
> not the result of chance. Still, the part left standing was so high that
> a palm tree seen from the top of it appeared no larger than a grass-
> hopper. It was also said that a person could walk for three days in
> the shadow of the Tower without ever leaving it. Finally—[…]—
> whoever looked upon the ruins of the Tower was believed to forget
> everything he knew. (p. 45)

Milton (1667), on the other hand, offers a different image:

> But God, who oft descends to visit men
> Unseen, and through their habitations walks
> To mark their doings, them beholding soon,
> Comes down to see their city, ere the tower
> Obstruct heav'n tow'rs, and in derision sets
> Upon their tongues a various spirit to raze

> Quite out their native language, and instead
> To sow a jangling noise of words unknown:
> Forthwith a hideous gabble rises loud
> Among the builders; each to other calls,
> Not understood, till hoarse, and all in rage,
> As mocked they storm; great laughter was in heav'n
> And looking down, to see the hubbub strange
> And hear the din; thus was the building left
> Ridiculous, and the work Confusion named.
> (*Paradise Lost*, XII, 48–62, pp. 445–446)

What was the objective of such an incredible feat? To forge a proper name for themselves, a name for humanity. Babel, Derrida explains, is *confusion* (regardless of the homophony of the original terms), but as Voltaire indicates in his *Dictionnaire philosophique*, it is also the City of God (Ba: Father; Bel: God) (Derrida, 1979, p. 166). It follows that humanity does not manage to acquire its proper name, but rather that God descends and gives them His own (He imposes and opposes); namely, *Confusion*, and from then on the confusion of tongues operates. And so, the name of God as name of the father, by giving His name and successively all names, gives origin to language. However, as Derrida further points out, "understanding is no longer possible when there are only proper names, and understanding is no longer possible when there are no longer proper names" (p. 167), resulting in the confusion of tongues in the city of Babel. The unpronounceable name of YHWH leads to the dispersion and proliferation of languages. It is the sole name of God as name of the father, the one that imposes the mark of language that is not capable of being appropriated, namely, its confusion.

As Walter Benjamin suggests, translation is law, imposing an insolvent debt that must be paid; it then "... becomes necessary and impossible, like the effect of a struggle for the appropriation of the name, necessary and forbidden in the interval between two absolutely proper names" (Derrida, 1979, p. 170). The name of God becomes confused in the language in such a way that it goes on to signify *confusion*. The notion of the proper name is in no way foreign to psychoanalysis and to a certain extent it could be said that it is a desirable result for a specific type of analysis that the analysand may acquire and enjoy a proper name. What does acquiring a proper name imply? That the name of the Other no longer operates in me as a measuring stick. There lies precisely the difference between overcoming the father and going beyond him. To surpass the father implies to join him in a phallic struggle that, even when triumphing over the father, can only lead to frustration and discomfort. (Is there a more phallic structure in ancient western narratives than the Tower of Babel itself?) Evidence of this is the chapter "Those wrecked by success" in Freud's work "Some character-types met with in psycho-analytic work" (1916d). To surpass the father implies that the father is no longer the phallus that serves as measure of the world but that the subject has been able to build one that is precisely his proper name. We know that this is not the sole virtue of psychoanalysis: the arts have revealed other processes and struggles, more or less painful, through which that name can be acquired.

What is interesting about Benjamin's thinking is that, when he reflects on the debt imposed by translation, he articulates the dimension of supply and demand in relation to the confusion of tongues; that is, what does an analysand demand with respect to his confusion of tongues? Does he demand a metalanguage which will *speak* to him in his alienation of the Other's word? Does he demand that the analyst re-establish that language of the Other, which through the symptom reveals its cracks? On the other hand, what does the analyst offer? An absolute language without the ruptures that the patient now complains of? Does he offer himself as subject of a supposed knowledge, bearer of the proper name by excellence? Ferenczi alerts us to the fact that what the patient demands is to return to the sleep of the Other's metalanguage, the profound sleep of meaning. With this in mind, the analyst has two options, both impossible: to offer him sleep or awakening. On the one hand, the analyst cannot offer a metalanguage (*Ursprache*), which is structurally lost; on the other, he cannot offer an awakening to the real because the latter is the place of the impossible. Nevertheless, it appears once again as the thread that leads to psychoanalysis, pulling it along an intermediate course. J. -A. Miller (1986) makes the following suggestion: "Awakening [to the real] is impossible if, as Lacan puts it, the unconscious implies that we not only dream when we are asleep. But psychoanalysis can inspire the wish of how this would be if it were possible" (p. 120). Benjamin thinks in a similar manner with respect to translation: it is lost before it even starts because the lack itself provoked by language makes it impossible for a language to exist that will allow absolute and essential translation to take place. However, says Benjamin, it is in the movement towards that absolute language, as an asymptote that does not touch the parallel, that language itself is enriched, producing the marvel that intermediate language inhabits. This Benjaminian reflection is absolutely coherent with his Jewish thought: the Jewish logic is not validated at the point at which the Messiah arrives, but rather in the waiting itself, of that promise of the end of all times, which produces the beauty in the movement towards that line of escape, towards that horizon, always unattainable. The analysand, for his part, in the movement towards the unblotted, towards the absolute, in that search for answers regarding what is happening to him, in the crusade to restructure an ego free from ruptures, comes up against the very center of his *Spaltung*, with the hole that constitutes him as a desiring being and from which the Name sprouts.

Going back to translation, we observe the autonomy of the translated work and of the original work. As we stated earlier, the subject of the translation acquires a debt (insolvent) with the work demanded by producing the translation. But the translated text is not an inscription of the same text in another language or a transformation of the codes of another language. It is above all another text; precisely "the bond or obligation of the debt does not pass between a donor and a donee but between two texts (two 'productions' or two 'creations')" (Derrida, 1979, p. 179). For this reason, translations acquire a life of their own and become independent texts. Granoff (1984) affirms that "Strachey produced nothing less than a competitive *de facto* work from Freud's. His work stands out over Freud's in the mental and psychic reading market. And over that of education" (p. 167). Willson (2004) states that "[a]ccording to Foucault, Hegel was so present in Hyppolite's translation that the Germans themselves resorted to it in order to understand what, 'for an instant at least, turned into the German version'" (p. 16). Translation, therefore, far from being an image or copy, does not appear as the representation or reproduction of that other text from which it departs.

For the translator, passing from one language to another appears as a feat that tends towards the absurd. But it does not always occur from one language to the other; sometimes there are many languages that speak in one, and the polyphony of the phrases overflows the possibilities given by the literality of the languages and their correspondence word for word. Thus, a particular semantic order registers a certain versatility in its multilingual resonance.

By way of example, we can see that the *he war* of Joyce's *Finnegans Wake*, also referred to by Derrida, signifies "war" in English and "was" in German. Similarly, the work's title can vary according to whether *Finnegans* is read with or without apostrophe, that is, as a possessive, as *Finn-again*, or if the *Wake* is read as funeral or as awakening (Boorstin, 1994, p. 648). How can this funeral and this awakening be thought about in relation to Ferenczi's role in the psychoanalytic movement, placing him on the side of awakening (*Ferenczi's Wake*)? Borges (1964) also links awakening with death:

> Mi voz, mi rostro, mi temor, mi suerte.
> ¡Ah, si aquel otro despertar, la muerte,
> Me deparara un tiempo sin memoria
> De mi nombre y de todo lo que he sido!
> ¡Ah, si en esa mañana hubiera olvido! (p. 272)

> [My voice, my face, my fear, my fortune./Oh, if that other awakening, death,/Would offer me a time without memory/Of my name and everything I've been!/Oh, if on that morning, oblivion were possible!]

Inversely, Borges (1984) will also link longevity with insomnia.

Returning to the linguistic value of Babel, we find that its Akkadian meaning seems to have been "Gateway to God". Such an etymological depiction of the word is traced by André Parrot in *The Tower of Babel* (1961), a journey that goes from the cuneiform texts about Ziggurats to the writings of Herodotus of Halicarnassus. The author undertakes, in turn, his own translation exercise, arguing that the word "babel" comes from the Hebrew tradition of "balal", meaning "to confuse" as well as "to mix". He further suggests that "it seems too directly and very probably copied from the Akkadian bab-ilu (door of god)" (Parrot, 1961, p. 14). This last meaning, not less significant, also has its roots and transcendence in the collective imagination of languages. For this reason, it is interesting to note that "Babel" is the same word today in a myriad of languages, since it reveals a particular dimension of proper names, as if they belonged to a different sphere from that of regular language; it pierces and at the same time deceives the senses, since at least Babel enjoys its double nature: being a proper name and a common name, name of God the father as well as *confusion*.[2] And it is even more confusion as *confusion* since, by its semantic correspondence (a kind of intra-linguistic translation), it becomes, in turn, a proper name;

namely, *Confusion* as the name of God the father. And that is why "…
a proper name as such remains forever untranslatable, a fact that may
lead one to conclude that it does not strictly belong, for the same reason
as the other words, to the language, …" (Derrida, 1979, p. 171). And it
only does so by letting itself be translated in its semantic meaning in the
language; therefore, the proper name is inscribed inasmuch as it ceases
to be proper.

According to Benet, in his text *The Construction of the Tower of Babel*
(1990), three myths about the tower, of autonomous and different
nature, come together: the existence of a unique race with one sole language; the intention of building a tower that would reach the heavens;
and the decision of the divinity to abort the project, of destroying the
Utopia, leading to a second expulsion from Paradise (p. 50). In this way,
the dimension of translation as one single text also appears, insofar as
one same text is subject to the production of a diversity of meanings.
And it is also the dimension of the text as inexhaustible, that is, capable
of being translated as many times as that which has been introduced
within it insists on.

CHAPTER EIGHT

Walter Benjamin's contributions to the issue of the "confusion of tongues"

"But where there is danger,
A rescuing element grows as well."

Hölderlin, quoted by Heidegger
(in Palnier & Towarnicki, 1981)

Benjaminian reflection regarding language is of infinite richness for this investigation, since it greatly contributes to thinking about the confusion of tongues, allowing us to study in depth what we have raised in relation to trauma and language in Sándor Ferenczi's work. Benjamin places language in the dimension of what is eminently human, in the sense that it is not possible to raise a question about man split off from the dimension of language. The latter is both the way in which man manages to express himself and the way in which what exists is expressed by man. Language in Benjamin is creative and the basis from which all knowledge about what is human departs. Nevertheless, even though he appeals to the unavoidable importance of the name, he will not let himself be deceived by the existence of a direct relationship between words and the beings of the world. It is on this point that Benjaminian reflection approaches the task of the poets.

As Mallarmé suggests, the contract between words and the world has been broken. An adjustment of the words to the beings of the world no longer exists. The task of the poet is above all creative; it consists of creating as many worlds as possible, acting as architect of a fictional world made of words and linguistic turns. Words do not limit themselves to the possibilities that the world offers and, at the same time, the world does not let itself be spoken by language, because it is precisely the correspondence of the word with the objects of the world, the relationship in which western metaphysics has placed so much trust, that crumbles with the fall of the fundamentals. The grammatical order of things no longer exists and the word is pure arbitrariness, the creative tool of poets, the last limit of an encounter with the other. "Mallarmé says no, words are the place where the world dwells, but not as the truth of the world but as the truth of language" (Forster, 2006). On the other hand, according to Hölderlin, it is none other than Hyperion who discovers the perverse logic according to which the totality of the logic of horror that has been unleashed is a result of man's frenetic search for liberty. Hyperion reveals that it is precisely the search for liberty that leads to the creation of the conditions of evil, violence, and confinement; it is in the logic of violence that the logic of horror unleashes itself. Benjamin is fascinated with that enigmatic phrase in Hölderlin's "Patmos": "But where there is danger, a rescuing element grows as well", and adapts it from its Messianic structure in order to think of catastrophe not as antagonistic to opportunity but precisely as what maintains possibility—as opportunity—within itself, according to that Kafkian logic where those who are desperate are precisely those to whom opportunity opens its doors. We observe that what is violent, barbaric, and irrational is not an outside, an alien, and exiled otherness, but is immersed instead in the subject of civilisation itself.

Foucault (1963), whose study of Raymond Roussel's work is probably still the most significant, analyses the parallel that the French poet makes between language and the sun: both spheres broken, always present but unattainable. In the last chapter of that atypical work, Foucault states:

> It *is* Roussel's linguistic space, the void from which he speaks, the absence which binds and mutually excludes his work and his madness. This void is not to be understood as a metaphor. It *is* the insolvency of words which are fewer in number than the things they designate, and due to this principle of economy must take on

meaning. (1963, pp. 166–167, italics in original; also taken up by Eribon, 1992, p. 201, in his study of Foucault)

The paradox that he raises in his analysis of Roussel was openly exposed by the poet himself: language borders on madness, since in its own retreat it weaves the void extracted from it. Foucault also provides the coordinates with Artaud's work, which constantly meanders along that void, in the permanent oscillation of approaching-disappearing from its object.

Among the issues that Ferenczi enunciates as "confusion of tongues", a kind of destroyed childhood appears caused by the other who speaks. With his words, the other blots out forever that original and mythical virginity that precedes speech. In this way, that which Ferenczi refers to as "language of tenderness" is a non-language, a primordial sea, *Thalassa*, where the perversion of the word has not yet made its entrance. This occurs due to the other, the imposition of a "language of passion", a language that articulates desire, filling the world with foreign signifiers. In that loss of the word, the child will search for a signifier that will name him amongst all those others that name *other* things.

Along these lines we can read the famous "The dream of the wise baby" (Ferenczi, 1923), which fascinated Ferenczi so much, in which a new born baby speaks. Ferenczi, who interprets the dream on the part of the wisdom of the baby or the small child that starts to speak on the couch and who knows about sexuality, affirms that his interpretation is incomplete. We may dare another interpretation, which is a human being who does not suffer the trauma of language, who does not have to start looking for his name in the Other's signifiers, but who has already incorporated them from the womb (he is already born with his Name). That immaculate child is precisely the structural position of the tender childhood as forever lost. On the other hand, the imposition of one tongue over another, pure confusion of tongues, is related to the types of language described by Benjamin.

In his work, Benjamin refers to different types of language, starting from the Kabbalistic concepts characteristic of his Jewish tradition. On the one hand, he is interested in what he calls "creative language"; the language characteristic of God, and His enunciation is, at the same time, creation. It is not a language used adjectivally, a language that offers descriptions of the world, but instead, in the very act of enunciation, it creates all the conditions of possibility of the world. This is characteristic of Talmudic thought, which conceives a world made of language and words. That unavoidable aspect of the world and language, as well as the overwhelming weight that the written word brings, is always present in Jewish thought. It is, in this context, that uncontaminated, *pre-babelian* language of confusion.

On the other hand, we have the nominative language of Adam, which goes back to the role he played in Eden as the one who gave each thing its rightful name. For Judaism, the world is a creation of the word, the word of God. Adam, as the first man, receives a donation that consists in giving each thing an appropriate name. Unlike God, Adam is not responsible for the creation of the order of things, but of something at a much lower level, at least in ontological terms, that has to do with a secret subtlety hidden in the silence of language. When he names things, Adam does not affirm the violence of language that supposes an arrangement over the order of things. Neither does it involve the use of conceptual language and the universal categories that force each thing to submerge to a greater order. There is no domination in the nominative language of Adam, but the possibility that each thing may appear in what each says of itself through its name. That donation, received by Adam, unfolds itself poetically as a gift of giving to each thing the name that each name speaks. Adam's gesture consists in giving the appropriate name to things; it is not a gesture of domination and appropriation, it is not the violence with which the possibility of each thing is limited, circumscribing it to one single way of being said (conceptual), but rather it consists of giving to each thing the name that speaks in it and which belongs to it.

Nevertheless, the named thing does not find in that word its own lived history, its experience in the world, because in Paradise, since there is no death, there is no history either. There is no time, no present, past, or future, no succession of parts, no before and after. History starts with the expulsion from Eden and with the confusion of tongues, with the loss of that unique and original language, *Ursprache*, which introduces the dimension of lack in the word of men. In that language, which previously allowed communication between all human beings, a fissure is now introduced, a rupture, a disagreement. But Benjamin does not find this catastrophic, or at least he does not see in that catastrophe the end of possibilities; on the contrary, in that confusion of tongues the possibility exists of increasingly enriching the word, not appealing to the proximity with a metalanguage, but in the auscultation of an interlanguage, which begins to find its way from the passing of one language to the other. This does not present a contradiction with respect to the way in which Ferenczi understands the confusion of tongues, but quite the opposite, since the confusion of tongues always plays with that double aspect: on the one hand, it can be castrating in the limiting sense and pathologically traumatic, and on the other, it is enabling and enriching. Always, on one level, it is traumatic because it corresponds to the loss produced by the word in all speaking beings, in the polymorphous perversion of speech, but it is in that structural hole that the[1] wealth of the human world, of the speaker, of the word expands.

The first two languages described, the creative and the nominative, aim at languages not pierced by the confusion of tongues. The first is a language that makes the world, the word is the thing itself; and the second is a language that presents no distance between words and things. As Benjamin points out, history is a result of the expulsion from Paradise, and it is only outside Eden's gates that language can become a succession of words that speak of the world. That significant linkage, which has a particular synchrony, is a result of the confusion of tongues. Here, we are once again before the paradox that can be read in Ferenczi's oeuvre: the confusion of tongues presents itself as an inevitable condition of every speaker and, at the same time, it is the traumatism where symptomatic productions simmer. It acquires the form of a transaction: handing over innocence in exchange for language in order to enter into a succession mobilised by the search for that innocence that is now lost forever.

Nevertheless, for Benjamin, there is a possible impoverished future for Babelian language. That language of confusion is a potentially enriched tongue, but loses its possibilities in the language of communication. The language of communication is one that is articulated in concepts—the presence of the *multiple* in the *one*. It is here where representational language finds its way; it is, above all, the language of violence, because it fixes immovable conditions on the possibility of allowing what is spoken to appear. This language of civilisation appeals to the silence of words. Levi-Strauss will oppose it to primitive language, the language of the savages. This "language of the savages, says the author of *Tristes Tropiques*, is a language which linguistically proliferates over the world, appropriating itself of the world's diversity and not reducing that diversity to a conceptual unity" (Forster, 2006, without page). But Benjamin does not give up in the face of the violence of the language of communication. Behind mechanisms of appropriation and silencing, the Name continues to vibrate, elevating its resonances.

With this in mind, Benjamin continues appealing to the search for the Name, inserting himself into the Kabbalistic tradition, but he does not do this in a naive way. He does not act like a mystic or an alchemist, searching for a lost language, the "language of the birds" (Benjamin, 1918, p. 74) that enounces the truth of each thing. Neither does he proceed in a delirious fashion, like Schreber with his *Grundsprache*, in communication without an other, with a double-headed God whose plan includes the restructuring of humanity. Benjamin does not alter his work because the Messiah has not arrived; he knows that the essence of his Judaism lies in the waiting. Instead, Benjamin chooses, among all languages, the intermediate language that never stops consolidating itself, which is always about to be broken by the word and which is the language enriched in translation. Thus, Benjamin gives a directive to assign a place to psychoanalytic language: the one that does not speak about what the subject *is*, his individuality in relation to a totality, his essence in relation to a foundation, or his nosology in relation to a psychiatric or scientific category; instead, psychoanalytic language lies in the display of the word in the analytic relationship, in the passing of the narratives that are the working material of the session, in those signifiers that come from the other and are the name of the other. The subject is gradually able, in each repetition, to give form to those new signifiers, which, without being alien to the other, speak—each time more frequently—of his own desire. The search for the Name is no more than a directive, what, for Ferenczi, mobilises the desire of the analyst. His search for the infant (for Ferenczi, the patient is always an infant who suffers on the couch) is a directive, starting from which that expatriated language begins to find its way over the language of the Other, which is why the subject finds himself exiled; and it is in this movement that the analysand arrives at an awakening. Let us remember that awakening to the real is impossible (since we do not dream only when we are asleep) and, nevertheless, it is in that direction that the analyst's desire moves and it is that desire that enables the analysand to exit from hypnosis.

Benjamin finds two possible ways of giving back the voice to the word that screams behind the silence of concepts. One is the poetic path, the ability that the poet has of extoling the possibilities of language, of taking the word to its limits, of listening to what is spoken within it, its demands, its possibilities, its skin. But there is another, deeper level of that nominative restitution: translation. For Benjamin (1918), "[t]ranslation is the transference of a language to another through a continuity of transformations. Translation entails a transformative continuity and not the comparison of abstract equalities or areas of resemblance" (p. 69). The work of the translator—which, since there is no way of being entirely loyal to the meaning when passing from one language to another is impossible from the start—tries to take full advantage of what the word silences, its coarser sounds. In an intermediate zone, in a place where the original language or source or target language no longer dwells but instead in the area of rupture, breakup, and fracture, the darkest sounds of language appear.

> It's in that interlanguage, in that short circuit where the substance of language, its grammatical fabric and morphology simultaneously light up because the translator discovers that language contains forgotten empathies, lost solidarities, a world devoid of meaning which translation puts back at the forefront. For Benjamin, the translator carries a redemption, that of language, of that loss of its nominative function, having fallen into a strictly representative function. (Forster, 2006, without page)

And what is revealed in this interlanguage? Above all, a place where the experience of the word (which Benjamin terms its spiritual dimension) is unpronounceable; an unbreakable limit of speech, which dwells like a treasure at the bottom of language. And, once again, the place of hope appears in Benjamin, since in that unutterable place, in that unreachable limit of the word, arises the promise of the unity of that significant and broken world. Let us remember that Ferenczi, according to what he describes in his *Clinical Diary* (1932b), also believed in the initial unity of his split patients: even in the severest psychotic split exists the promise of unity. Earlier, in his *Thalassa: A Theory of Genitality* (1924a), Ferenczi had referred to an original and mythical state that preceded the cycle of catastrophes that result in the apparition of sexuality. *Thalassa*, that primordial sea, is the place where desire soundly sleeps, without any possibility of awakening.

Benjamin does not want to produce a translation that speaks with the words of a lost unity, that is, in the restitution of unmistakable languages, but rather the promise of unity is there as a motor and an insurmountable barrier; and it is in that approach before the impossible (Real)—that which guides all attempt at translation—that the possibility is raised of blowing up the limits of all words and all language, lifting up that voice of the name that will never exhaust itself but which makes of it, its uniqueness, its multiplicity. The kind of translation that attempts to accommodate itself to the original is, above all, silence, language of domination, representational silence of the infinite of speech. Benjamin escapes this. Psychoanalysis does not find its place there either: the patient does not come to be named by the analyst, or, at least, will not receive from the analyst the satisfaction of that demand. On the contrary, he comes to liberate himself from that Name of the Other, from that language of passion that has marred his innocence; and knowing that his innocence is lost is an arduous, grieving process. But it is on the road towards that innocence, starting from the language of passion, that the interlanguage will start to open up, making it possible to articulate the exiled desire and leading towards an awakening *to* the confusion of tongues. There is no awakening *from* the confusion of tongues: that would imply falling into the sound sleep of a metalanguage. Literature presents us with examples of this. When Hölderlin translates Sophocles, he does not want to transcribe the Greek plays into the corresponding German voices; instead, he makes them talk in an intermediate language that belongs neither to Greek nor to German, but extols the promise of unity that silences in words, speaking through the weaving of that interlingual bridge. Along these lines, analytic language also appears as a *daimonic* tongue, because psychoanalysis, just like love—according to the teachings of Diotima, the wise woman of Mantinea (Plato, 1962)—is also something in-between.

The presence of hope in Benjamin's discourse is compelling. Even though entry into history is entry into death, into civilisation's distress, the pain of barbarism, the violence of imposition, the misplacement of what is lost, injustice, there exists nevertheless the promise, awaited since the beginning of time, of what the word does not pronounce. It is in this regard that reminiscence in Benjamin is perhaps the projection of that Messianic promise. Remembering does not mean surveying the immobility of what has occurred but instead renovating the light that projects towards the future, like the hope that is to come.

Benjamin establishes a very particular way of relating to the past, introducing it into his thought. He never regards the past with the air of an antiquary, as if he were observing relics in a museum; on the contrary, every glance towards a past event necessarily implies a new regard that resignifies that event. Consequently, a permanent transformation of past events is evoked in order to reflect upon the present, and the current state of affairs is, in turn, transformed by those evoked occurrences. That is why Benjamin is interested in the unfulfilled dreams of humanity, in its toys, in its childhood, in child fantasies as a place of the archaic, the uncontaminated, the multiple. Here we are reunited, once again, with Ferenczi. The interest in childhood is not an attempt to compile the narration of childhood, the originally traumatising scene that will liberate the analysand from trauma. The immaculate childhood is the guideline, the suspicion that where there appears to be a culmination of the Other's citations there is, in fact, a subject who chooses to enunciate those citations. Benjamin had a project for many years: constructing a work made up only of citations, of the words and phrases of others. He knew that in that work his word was above all the one that spoke, as also did Borges (1944) in his "Pierre Menard, author of the Quixote", who knew that the author was not incurring any plagiarism whatsoever.

It is for this reason that Benjamin thinks of history in allegorical rather than symbolic terms. While he regards the symbol as rigid and immovable, enjoyer of immediate significations, allegory appears to him as the very evidence of what is fragmentary, and, accordingly, carries with it a multiplicity of meanings. In his study of German Baroque writers of the seventeenth century, Benjamin observes the way in which language expresses an eminently fragmentary period. And the beauty derived from his reflection is that each of those fragments is, in itself, a promise of totality, of completeness, but not in the way of the symbol, which is immovable totality, but as a promise always forthcoming, located in that hopeful, Messianic future. Benjamin's idea is profoundly Ferenczian in relation to the *splitting* and to the clinical practice of fragmentation undertaken by the Hungarian analyst (see Gutiérrez-Peláez, 2006).

The theme of experience in Benjamin is linked with translation insofar as in it also lies an unbreakable frontier. There is a dimension of *experiencing* not made available to words, but which keeps its place in a beyond from which it insists. Benjamin notes this in the soldiers who return from the trenches during the First World War. For these traumatised soldiers, language had collapsed and died in that bloodbath, with eight or nine million dead and six million invalided. The articulation is maintained, therefore, according to which one of the effects of trauma is always the loss of the word, even in the confusion of tongues, since its most benign aspect, like the acquisition of language, implies at the same time the loss of signifiers and the shipwreck of what a language of tenderness is. In the war trauma, for example, due to the radical and unique nature of that experience, soldiers became mute.

In his essay "The storyteller", Benjamin (1936) expresses his thoughts on this subject in the following terms:

> With the [First] World War a process began to become apparent which has not halted since then. Was it not noticeable at the end of the war that men returned from the battlefield grown silent— not richer, but poorer in communicable experience? What ten years later was poured out in the flood of war books was anything but experience that goes from mouth to mouth. (p. 362)

What made evident the muteness that characterised the soldiers who returned from the trenches was the impossibility of dealing symbolically with the experiences suffered. A dimension of the incommunicability took refuge in experience. The vast literary production triggered by the horrors of war was not the transcription of what the victims narrated but rather a cultural attempt, from the perspective of art, to inscribe a footprint of that impossibility against which the word stumbled.

This, however, is not the tragic dimension of language; it is not the absence of words that operates as nucleus of the trauma—the trauma-tising value is in the war—, but quite the reverse: it is in that dimension of the unpronounceable that irrigates the value of the experience itself. Trauma, in any event, imprints that unique nuance of all experience and it is in the process of delving into that mute zone that the narrative of what occurred gradually nourishes that experience with truth. What would make the experience traumatic would be not to make it speak, or fencing it in the silence of the generality of the trauma, in the universality that the horror of war entails in each of those young men who returned with their body or *pneuma* torn, who killed or saw their friends killed. Trauma is strengthened in its destruction if it is silenced, if what is said within it is not heard, to the extent that it becomes law. Experience will always be a "beyond": beyond the law, beyond the totality, beyond concepts, beyond the words of language. Experience in no way exhausts itself in meaning, but flows in that dimension of human frailty that narrates the uniqueness of what has taken place.

In psychoanalysis, Winnicott will start with Ferenczi in order to speak of the need to experience in analysis, for the first time, the trau-matic event that occurred during infancy and which, given the prema-ture condition of the child's psyche, could not be incorporated within the field of experience itself. In this to and fro of the traumatic, each form of experience leaves behind a remainder, a dimension of what occurred that is not added to a totality, which does not subsume itself to the ways of knowing employed by the mechanisms of reason. But "Be careful!" Benjamin warns; we are not appealing to the essence of the experience but to that which allows the experience to *be*, despite what can be said of it. What lives inside the experience is not the muteness of the *eidos*, its *quiddity*. That would imply bringing to wakefulness once again the dormant gods that make thought submerge itself once more in its own dreams. Benjamin appeals in no way to an essentialism, but instead to the radical difference that dwells in experience; not the one that makes it equal to itself, but, on the contrary, the one that is always an exceptional state, which does not add to a totality but is always remainder, and in that remnant the promise of unity insists to the end of time (which, of course, never occurs; that is its messianic condition).

When Benjamin brings to the fore the daydreams of men through the ages, he does it with a sole purpose, articulated with Ferenczian ways of proceeding: he does so to promote an awakening from the deep sleep that drags the thought of sameness and totality. That is why Benjamin searches in the remnants, in the pieces, in the fragments, because in them—and not in the museum-like regard that reviews the immobility of history behind the firmness of crystals—lies the promise of a reconciliation. And he undoubtedly knows that there is no guarantee whatsoever of that promise, that the fragments become dispersed at each step, that the waves are finally silenced over the lake and the dreams forgotten with the end of night and the arrival of day. But, as Forster (2006) affirms:

> without the effort of remembrance, without listening once again to the forgotten narratives, without listening to the unpronounceable of language, certain destiny, its only guarantee, will be barbarism. Probably this will continue to occur and we will go on losing the opportunity of remembering that which we forget. But, says Benjamin, since history is not only a necessary, homogeneous and linear accumulation of events that take us towards the future but, rather a surprise, an uneasiness, a state of catastrophe, of exception, perhaps without guarantees, that unarmed subject, lost of himself, expropriated, fragmented, might find in the other—as Lévinas would say much later—an opportunity. (Without page)

It is there, in the fragments, in the remnants of the world, that Benjamin, like a recycler, roams with his cardboard texts the untrodden corridors of history and the crevices through which men do not dare to pass, covering their ears and averting their gaze; humanity knows that there, inside each piece, and not in the totality, it might be possible to recognise that fragment as its own; thus awaiting that utopia of lost reconciliation.

For Benjamin, the text does not produce its receivers and translators, but requires and claims them in the place where the law is imposed—the law of translation (always unsuccessful)—, and it is there that a dimension is opened to think about the analytic demand. The analysand appears in this regard like a *to-be-translated*, not by the analyst as representation, but by the place he occupies in relation to the analytic device. What is essential in this demand for translation does not travel the path of what is said, enounced, communicated, or even of the topic. Derrida's reading of Benjamin offers a view on translation, starting from the sacred text, where communication is not essential. "But what does a literary work [*Dichtung*] 'say'? What does it communicate? Very little to those who understand it" (quoted by Derrida, 1979, p. 181). Thus, when Winnicott (1954), upset because of the badly interpreted statement that "the analyst is an artist", asks himself "what patient would be interested in being the poem or the picture of someone else?" (p. 394), it is worth explaining that it is not as a creation of the analyst—that is, as production of the words enounced by him, since this would mean going back to hypnosis and sleep—but as understood in the equalisation of languages—in that displaced convergence of one language with another, the patient's and the one belonging to the analyst—where something of the patient's own voice (of his name) can be recovered. The demand of translation is given even before the translator appears; we could say that it is present in the structure of the original. The debt is not forcing the presentation of a copy or a loyal version of the original. Neither is the analyst obliged to represent or to communicate; nevertheless, an analytical agreement exists that assigns and forces both parts. If, as Lacan suggests, the unconscious is structured like a language, a translation of what it *says* must be made. The very nature of the unconscious, incessantly pushing, contains in itself various elements that go hand in hand with that which Benjamin terms the *to-be-translated*.

The original does not appear fixed in time, but is also subject to the laws of mutation, of the future and of multiple transformations.

The original gives itself in modifying itself; this gift is not an object given; it survives and lives on in mutation: "For in its survival, which would not merit the name if it were not mutation and renewal of something living, the original is modified. Even for words that are solidified there is still a post-maturation.". (Derrida, 1979, p. 183)

The idea of mutation of the original, its modification, suggests for psychoanalysis—even if this is not Derrida's intention, at least not in this essay—the possible multiplicity of analytical interventions. Thus, the word will always exist and the text will not be silenced. The question is placed in terms of which analytical interventions make possible mobilisations towards sleep (sense) and which towards awakening (effect); in this respect, it is essential to keep in mind Ferenczi's technical innovation as a movement towards the possibility of awakening. The aim of analysis, if we consider analysis as translation, would not be given by the analysand's identification with the analyst, since translation is not reproduced, but increases with its own capacity to speak for itself, different to a son who subjects himself to the law of reproduction. The latter is precisely what is on the side of hypnosis; the ability to speak—by oneself, to the extent that it is different—would, on the contrary, be on the side of dehypnotising.

Benjamin is interested in the kinship between languages, not as a historian but rather as one who examines the enigmatic relationship that results between one language and another. "A translation would not seek to say this or that, to transport this or that content, to communicate such a charge of meaning, but to re-mark the affinity among the languages, to exhibit its own possibility" (Derrida, 1979, p. 186). If the original demands translation, it is understood from the start that in itself, despite its value as an original, it is not in a state of completeness. The original is also pierced by lack and finds itself in dissymmetry even with itself, since the laws of identity do not apply to it either. Consequently, it is understood that the translator, like the analyst, if we follow the metaphor of analyst as translator,

... must redeem (erlösen), absolve, resolve, in trying to absolve himself of his own debt, which is at bottom the same—and bottomless. "To redeem in his own tongue that pure language exiled in the foreign tongue, to liberate by transposing this pure language captive in the work, such is the task of the translator." (Derrida, 1979, p. 188)

So, in this interplay, language is made to grow. It appears not as an iron structure but in a fugitive way, just as the contact between what the analyst says and analytical interpretation is also fugitive (what is fugitive—as point of encounter—is interpretation itself). Benjamin provides the metaphor of the tangent that only touches the circle at an infinitely small point of meaning, which is the meeting place between translation and the original, between the analyst and the analysand, and is, at the same time, what permits the movement of that line extending into the infinite. At the end of that journey, just as we conceive of the line finding itself in the infinite to consolidate a circle (that is, also a promise, despite the specific features of mathematics in relation to translation), thus, as in fiction, a limit is placed before analysis and translation, but only inasmuch as it facilitates understanding, since by its very nature such a journey never ends.[1] And the bottom line of that proposed opening, which in the case of the analytic proposal deprives it of the image, is that it does not contradict the unity.

CHAPTER NINE

The death of God and the "language of the birds"

> "I would certainly never advise you to pursue the bizarre con-
> ceit which has taken hold of you to follow the dream about uni-
> versal language."
>
> Francesco Soave, *Riflessioni intorno all'istituzioned'una*
> *lengua universale, 1774* (epigraphed in Eco, 1993)

In the pages that follow, we will discuss two different visions of language. On the one hand, we will consider what the ancient mystics
called the "language of the birds", used to define a divine language,
known only to the initiated by illumination and free from the vicissitudes of the Babelian confusion. On the other, we have the Nietzschean
concept of "the death of God", which is of interest as *death of representa-*
tion. Taking these two notions into account will allow us to position the
logic of language we are trying to rescue in order to link the thinking of
Levinas and Benjamin with Ferenczi's notions of "childhood" and the
"confusion of tongues".

A means of circumventing the Babelian confusion seems to be offered
by the *language of the birds*. Far from positioning itself in the universalisa-
tion of language, the language of the birds is placed above all languages
and all translations. It is the very landmark of the word in its essence.

Regardless of the phenomenal materiality of the world, the language of the birds does not offer any distance between words and things; to a certain extent, in it the word *is* the thing. The role of Adam in Paradise is worth remembering: giving a name to divine creations (we should keep in mind the difference Benjamin establishes between God's "creative language" and the "nominative language" of Adam).

What do we know of this enigmatic language? According to tradition, whether mystic or religious, before the babelisation of language there existed the language of the birds. Fulcanelli (1922) says that

> *argot* (cant) is one of the forms derived from the *Language of the Birds*, parent and doyen of all other languages—the one spoken by philosophers and *diplomats*. It was knowledge of this language which Jesus revealed to his Apostles, by sending them his spirit, the Holy Ghost. This is the language which teaches the mystery of things and unveils the most hidden truths. The ancient Incas called it *Court Language*, because it was used by diplomats. To them it was the key to the *double science*, sacred and profane. In the Middle Ages, it was called the *Gay Science* and the *Gay Knowledge*, the *Language of the Gods*, the *Dive-Bouteille*. Tradition assures us that men spoke it before the building of the *Tower of Babel*, which event caused this sacred language to be perverted and to be totally forgotten by the greater part of humanity. (p. 44, italics in original)

We also know that Tiresias, who for seven years lives the experience of femininity and possesses the gift of telling the future, knows something about the *language of the birds*, the language that helps to avoid the obstacles of the Babelian confusion. This is the same language that Christ supposedly taught his disciples. Let us remember that, according to Eco (1997), "*in Christo non est masculus neque faemina*" (p. 20); that is, also in Christ we see the interplay present in Tiresias between language and femininity. The blind prophet knew this tongue, taught to him by the goddess Minerva. Fulcanelli (1922) affirms that "[m]ythology would have it that the famous soothsayer Tiresias had perfect knowledge of the *Language of the birds*, which Minerva, goddess of Wisdom, revealed to him. He shared it, they say, with Thales of Miletus, Melampus and Appolonius of Tyana" (p. 44).

Athena's words to the serpent Ericthonius also resonate: "Clean Tiresias' ears with your tongue so that he may comprehend the language of the prophetic birds" (Graves, 1985, vol. 2, p. 10). What Tiresias reveals is that interesting dimension between translation and femininity, since it is precisely the impossibility he finds of talking about his *being a woman* and the clumsiness of his words that brings about his blindness as punishment. Some traditions affirm that Saint Francis of Assisi also delved into its mysteries: "Await here by the road while I go and preach to my small brothers the birds" (1390, Ch. XVI). Siegfried, the hero of the third opera in Wagner's cycle, *The Ring of the Nibelung*, understands the language of the birds after tasting the blood of Fafner, the dragon he has killed with his sword.

It is important to keep in mind what was stated in the previous chapter, namely, that the value of truth Benjamin offers to translation is far from wanting to be placed in harmony with a metalanguage; nor does he want to assign to a language the value of a metalanguage. Neither did Heidegger (1955) assign Greek to that position when he affirmed that "in the Greek language what is said is at the same time eminently that which what is said names" (p. 25). We note how that interest can lead *ad absurdum* in the example that Benet (1990) provides quoting Frazer who, in turn, resorts to Leibniz, affirming that:

> There are as many motives to believe that Hebrew was the original language of humanity as there are to adopt the opinion of Goropius who, in his book published in Antwerp in 1580, tried to prove that Dutch was the language spoken in Paradise. Another writer maintained that Adam had spoken in Basque while others, anticipating the very Scriptures, introduced the confusion of languages already in Eden, thus affirming that Adam and Eve spoke in Persian, that the serpent had spoken in Arabic and that the amiable archangel Gabriel had spoken with our first fathers in Turkish: there was even a writer who seriously held that the Almighty had addressed Adam in Swedish, that Adam had answered in Danish to his Maker and that the serpent had tempted Eve in French. (p. 59).

Thomas Moore also proposes an artificial universal language, a mixture of Hebrew, Greek, and Persian in his island of *Utopia*. Eco (1993), for his part, has been clear when he affirms that "[t]he topic of the confusion of tongues and the attempt to remedy it by recuperating or inventing a common language for the human race appears in the history of all cultures (p. 12).

As previously explained, the truth value of a translation, for Benjamin, is not in the way in which it loyally accommodates itself to the model from which it departs, nor in the adaptation to the meaning displayed by the original. What the text to be translated demands is not in the order of representation; what is required is rather the production of a greater language. Such is the promise that the exercise of translation undergoes, which vitiates the existence of a divine language, a metalanguage, or *language of the birds*, since that infinite and tiny point of what cannot be translated—so distant from the essence of the text, close to the notion of *nucleus* stated by Abraham (Derrida, 1997)—is precisely what enables the production of those other texts that are the multiple translations of one same original.

We could consider, as Abraham does, the presence of an unthinkable in the interior of languages, and there lies its interest before the paradox of: "'How can we include in a discourse, whichever it might be, that which, by its nature, would escape from it by its very essence?'" (Derrida, 1997, p. 73), which is precisely what there is of non-discourse in that discourse, what escapes the possibilities of translation and the possibilities of being represented. The original is not the archetype of the others; the original is also different from itself, as the original's translations are, despite the existing relationship between languages. Even if Fulcanelli (a name which, in its turn, translates as "Vulcan") affirms that the language of the birds is "court language", it so happens that it is a language that does not allow any cut[1] whatsoever; this is the distance that makes possible the production of translations and the production of a larger language. It is the cut that, according to Agamben (2005), *profanes* language, that is, that steals it from the gods and returns it to men for its just use.

When Nietzsche affirms that God is dead, it is understood that from the fall of the deity the fall of fundamentals will follow; all the fundamentals, in fact, since it is not a question of erecting new ones in God's place. The tomb of God must be kept empty and all that has found its place in that hole is a repetition of the same and not of what is different. Whether it be atheism, religiosity, philosophy, science, the body, etc., even though it is announced from a counterposition, from counterculture, from the adverse current or the opposite shore, it will not do otherwise than repeat what it is rebelling against. But silence does not follow from this. As Derrida (1998) affirms: "No doubt that Nietzsche called for an active forgetting of Being: it would not have the metaphysical form imputed to it by Heidegger" (p. 136).

Even though the emptiness of the foundation of being is revealed, the subject as fiction continues to be a philosophic tool, without implying, by this, the resurrection of the dead.

The absence of a foundation broadens the path of multiplicity; it frees the original from a translation that is its version in another language. A multi-voice of signifiers, intra- and extra- lingual, opens up. Thus, amid the limits of the word, Fulcanelli (1922) decrees at the end of his work: "Keep silent" (p. 177). Milton asked himself in *Paradise Lost* (1667):

> ... for who, though with the tongue
> Of Angels, can relate, or to what things
> Liken on earth conspicuous, that may lift
> Human imagination to such highth
> Of Godlike power?

When Wittgenstein (1922) attacked metaphysics, he approached it from another perspective: "Whereof one cannot speak, thereof one must be silent" (p. 90). But we note that precisely that which escapes the word must be pursued in all the nooks and crannies, the fissures, surrounding the obscure zones from whence it escapes, and, thus cornered, there steals from it a vague perfume, like the one produced by the Doppler effect, similar to a wave, the breath and memories of the receding body. Translation does not transcend language,

> ... it is not a reality which they [languages] would besiege from all sides, like a tower that they would try to surround. No, what they are aiming at intentionally, individually and jointly, in translation is the language itself as a Babelian event, a language that is not the universal language in the Leibnizian sense, a language which is not the natural language that each remains on its own either; it is the being-language of the language, tongue or language *as such*, that unity without any self-identity, which makes for the fact that there are languages and that they are languages. (Derrida, 1985, p. 201, italics in original)

Translation presents itself as a *being in harmony* of languages and texts, without any ambitions of completeness or totality.

Benjamin's language of truth appears distanced from what "court language" or the "language of the birds" is. The death of God as death of all foundation is, at the same time, the death of a universal language. In the absence of an "archetypal language", there is no last reference of meaning for the signifiers, but, on the contrary, meaning is what is displayed between words and things. There is no metaphysics of translation; no metalanguage. But there, precisely, lies the gift, because the multiplicity of voices and of meanings is what gives origin to the metaphor, to the play of language and the diversity of meanings. In the language of psychosis, a use of the word appears that does not allow these games of language and therefore is closer to that "literality" that the language of God or the language of the birds would condemn, or in any case, to the language that would have existed before the Babelian confusion and which would lead Ferenczi (1932b) to affirm that "God is insane, the world is chaotic" (p. 160). Thus a relationship is opened up between the word as death of the thing and God as death. God as death appears in the words of Sgalambro (1996): "To desire the common good is to desire no one's death, that is all. (How can we reconcile, I repeat, the idea of goodness with God, who is death itself? I think, on the other hand, that the idea of God and the idea of death are associated in such a way that we can use one name just as much as the other)" (p. 116).[2] *Death* would appear then like another name of God or like one more meaning of the unpronounceable YHWH. The death of God, on the other hand, would lead to never having to silence the word. The originals, says Benjamin, are not rocks or planets; they speak and transform themselves. They are not sold into immobility, and nourish themselves with what speaks of and for them in the proliferation of tongues. If we continue with the metaphor of psychosis, that is, of that state in which there is no metaphor, we end up encountering beings who are dead though alive: "the mentally sick are really half-dead people" (Ferenczi, letter to Groddeck dated 10 October 1930, quoted by Stanton, 1997, p. 47). It is worth remembering how Beckett, with the genius of his word, defended himself against this: "I've always had the impression that deep inside I was a murdered being. Killed before I was even born. I had to find that murdered being. Try to give him back his life" (Juliet, 2006).

In aphorism 125 of *The Gay Science* (1882) entitled "The madman", Nietzsche expresses for the second time in his work (the first was in "Prisoners", in his book *The Wanderer and his Shadow*, 1880), and in a very direct fashion, his concept of the death of God. These views appear through the words of a madman who approaches a multitude that do not believe in God and screams unceasingly: "I'm looking for God! I'm looking for God!" The crowd mocks him and at this point he reveals to them the state of that God who is dead. Furthermore, he tells them that humanity itself has killed God with its own knife, and is now tainted with divine blood. He then proceeds thus:

> "Where is God?" he cried; "I'll tell you! *We have killed him*—you and I! We are all his murderers. But how did we do this? How were we able to drink up the sea? Who gave us the sponge to wipe away the entire horizon? What were we doing when we unchained this earth from its sun? Where is it moving to now? Where are we moving to? Away from all suns? Are we not continually falling? And backwards, sideways, forwards, in all directions? Is there still an up and a down? Aren't we straying as though through an infinite nothing? Isn't empty space breathing at us? Hasn't it got colder?" (p. 120)

His words reveal that the pivot and angular axis of the earth's rotation has lost its centre and the earth has ceased to be the indelible rock of inalterable soundness; on the contrary, the surfaces reveal themselves as horrifyingly contemptible. The place of God has been left empty, drained, his body decomposes, and the complementary parts of the corruptible world have disappeared with the dissolving of the hereafter (Divine), which consolidated that perfect circle that the security of a flawless mechanism offered.

The death of God is the death of all truth as foundation. With that phrase, Nietzsche decrees an explosion and a fragmentation of truth, turning it into no more than a narrative or a fable. Truth now becomes

> an adventure of language, a conflict of words, a historical construc-
> tion, a violence through which someone imposes his own view of
> the world. Truth, therefore, does not drag a content of objectivity,
> an essence, it's not substantive, it doesn't respond to a fundamental
> but rather it emerges from the conflict of opposite views, of what
> Nietzsche also calls perspective, from what emerges in that con-
> flictive, violent and passionate convergence of different outlooks.
> Truth becomes separated from the fundamental, bursting all essen-
> tialism in order to affirm itself in historical materiality, to emerge
> from the battle of opposite views. (Forster, 2006, without page)

The explosion that operates through Nietzsche blurs all attempts to replace a first principle as the foundation of truth or as the consistency of being.

Now, what are we to do with the place of God, with that place that has been left empty? Nietzsche will say that the tomb of God (which is a tomb because it is the place where the divine body lies) must be left empty and, in his own way, explains how everything that will be placed there, whether it be to seal the emptiness or to make vain attempts to fill the void, will achieve nothing more than reviving and repeating that which implied the existence of God; it will prevent us seeing that killing God is the "most grandiose action". And if "[t]he greatness of that act is not too big for us?" (Nietzsche, 1882, p. 136). Deleuze will use this image to describe what happens with revolutions that, once they reach power, are trapped by the apparatus of capture, proceeding to do exactly that which they had protested against in the first place. The active and reactive forces annihilate themselves, just as man ceases to exist when he kills God; only when he dies as a result of taking life is the advent of the Superman possible (Deleuze, 1967). Regarding the issue at hand, we are interested in that spot whose healing is impossible; it is a cut that cannot even locate itself as such; there is no ulcer or scar, it is an open door. If we insert a finger in it we will only feel the edges, but nothing of the vacuum that inhabits it, which is not intelligible: the non-correspondence of the signifiers opens the road to the multiplicity of translations.

With respect to the psychoanalytic dimension, the same issue arises, since, in the presence of the patient's loss of meaning, endowing his existence with new meanings by way of the analytic device is, somehow, taking the patient once again towards sleep (of meaning), distancing him from awakening. That is why the notion of "effect of meaning", suggested by Lacan, is useful, since it maintains coherence with what has been proposed in relation to the wish of the analyst as the wish to guide the patient towards an awakening.

In Nietzsche's concepts, the most significant dimension that must be highlighted is the death of God as death of representation. The death of God implies the loss of the (ultimate) signifiers. It is a whole world of absolutes, of essences and transcendental values, that decomposes in the body of God. The words Nietzsche makes the madman utter refer to that hesitation implied by being in the place of lack, before that for which there are no words, and which lives in the region of the unnameable. It is the world of representation that has fallen. The name of God

(Father) is a signifier that does not refer to another signifier but to a void; it implies the functioning of a zero and this is the reason for its unnameable place. When Nietzsche suggests that "logic is no more than the chains of language" (quoted by Derrida, 1998, p. 216), he affirms that metaphysics has penetrated so far within the architecture of the grammatical processes that it seems that dispensing with them would lead to the impossibility of thinking. Reason itself, and the use philosophy makes of it, is inevitably mounted, for Nietzsche, on metaphysical categories. Being able to think forwards from the death of God implies renouncing those categories or accepting them as fictions.

The death of God in turn touches another edge, another nerve, because, as Freud clearly puts it, there is no psychic representation of death. Here there is also the brush of the tangent with its circle, so like that between Nietzsche and Freud without either of them affirming it. Nevertheless, it is a fact that their discoveries intertwine and find themselves in each other. As Freud himself asserted in his autobiographical study (1925d): "Nietzsche, another philosopher whose guesses and intuitions often agree in the most astonishing way with the laborious findings of psycho-analysis, was for a long time avoided by me on that very account; I was less concerned with the question of priority than with keeping my mind unembarrassed ..." (p. 60).[3] In that relationship between death and silence, Freud (1926d) affirms that there is something non-transferable in aesthetic and sexual enjoyment as well as in death. The death drive is mute and for this reason God dies in silence, with such little fuss that the majority of men have not realised it: "But when Zarathustra was alone he spoke thus to his heart: 'Could it be possible? This old saint in the forest has not yet heard anything of this, that God is dead!'"(Nietzsche, 1883–85).

The multiple possibilities for translations of an original is because they cohabit and, despite their diversity, misinterpretations do not—necessarily—dwell in them. The language of fundamentals can only find in translations versions or copies—bad ones—of the original (as were the things of the world in relation to archetypes, *eidos*). Above all, "[t]ranslation promises a kingdom to the reconciliation of languages" (Derrida, 1985, p. 200). That is the Messianic promise at the end of time offered by Benjamin. It is an extension to the infinite that leads to the encounter with the other, enabling each language to abandon its cloistered solitude, its own growth in that encounter with another tongue, which is what allows translation to take place. Thus, babelisation, far from appearing as a punishment, shows itself as a gift leading to an encounter with the different; it liberates us from Paradise, archetype of sameness, where each thing is just like itself and there is no distance between words and things. "Adam and especially Eve, have the original merit of having liberated us from paradise; our sin is that we yearn to return there" (Zuleta, 1980, p. 10). In other words, the sin of the subject is that he lives with the illusion of returning to that primitive state without accepting that the adult, with his seduction, has given him his liberation. Here we once again run into that positive element of the confusion of tongues, consistent with its Möbian movement: trauma that limits, trauma that liberates; trauma before which we sleep or before which we awake.

We may conclude, therefore, that the analysand will not understand anything about himself if the language imposed is that of the analyst over his own; it would be a *confusion of tongues*, like a lulling of sense. The analysand must understand the effects language has on him, the other in himself, and not appeal to the self. This is what Abraham suggests for the reading of his book *The Shell and the Kernel: Renewals of Psychoanalysis* (Abraham & Torok, 1994): "nothing will be understood if this text isn't read like he himself teaches us to read, keeping in mind the 'scandalous anti-semantics', that of 'de-signified concepts in virtue of the psychoanalytic context'. This text must be deciphered, therefore, with the help of the code he suggests and which belongs to his own writing" (Derrida, 1997, p. 71). The words of the analysand in turn are presented to be read in his own code and with the tools that appear there in his discourse. In analysis, rather than reading the text that is the words of the analysand, a translation is implied and demanded: reading them is, from the start, translating them.

CHAPTER TEN

The other "other" in Levinas

The lanterns of reason have not been able to illuminate the other with the light of sameness that makes of their faces a mask. Behind these masks, behind those *personae*, the *per-sound* of the other filtrates, not the other of me, but the other *other* who sings in the silenced choir through the thundering pipe organs of sameness: "You will not kill me, you will not confine me within your own radius of sameness. Do not kill me: do not make of me a representation." He who chants that song is a Lithuanian Jew born between two years and two worlds, between BC and AD, in the *between* of two periods according to the temporal totalitarianism imposed by the cult of Julius Caesar and Gregory XIII, which is, at the same time, the fine line that demarcates religious orthodoxy from the globalisation of all time. It is this Jew who realises that the otherness continues to be unthought of, despite the fact that his contemporaries feel it has already found its place in the thought of the *différance*. But it remains on the outside of that thought of the difference—which does not stop it from producing glimmers of a sameness that demarcates a frontier that excludes an outside, that is, the existence of an alterity inasmuch as sameness excludes, and, therefore, sameness continues to be the measuring rod of what is different, an other *other*, unthought of, whose countenance beckons me.

This author, Levinas, is interesting to think about with regard to the issue of the "confusion of tongues" in Ferenczi, because, although from another place, he attempts a mode of inquiry in philosophy that tries to account for that other, prior to the babelization of tongues. With his delicate use of philosophical language, he sets out to discover something about that other prior to the categories of language, that language of sameness through which the things of the world are named. Ultimately, Levinas attempts to rescue that difference of the other prior to the traumatism involved in the language of the Other. Once again, we come across the paradox that brings with it the confusion of tongues: with the entrance into language that the acquisition of the Other's signifiers implies, the *other* becomes lost. A shipwreck of the other takes place because the way of naming it will always be the language of sameness. The language of sameness is the language of the Other, of signifiers' Others. In this way, according to Levinasian thought, we come across Ferenczi's question once again: How can we know something of that other who is suffering on the couch? How can we rescue him from the language of the Other that has imposed itself in such a way that it has silenced the analytical subject? How can we make that innocent child, that language of tenderness, speak in the sessions? What can we do to make that structurally lost place, which is a motor of desire, find its articulation in the Other's signifiers so that it will be the subject who speaks?

Levinas, as well as Ferenczi, knows that place is lost; it is impossibility that inspires meaning in the work of both. Consequently, the search for that place operates as a directive: this guideline is what keeps the promise of the encounter with what is lost, but it is an encounter that never occurs in time. This is where Jewish temporality gains importance: waiting for a Messiah that never arrives. Meaning is placed in the search of an encounter that will never take place. Meaning is the expectation, not the encounter. Similarly, Ferenczi is moved in his clinical work by the promise of an encounter with that uncontaminated place of trauma, prior to all traumatism. In addition, when Ferenczi finds himself in his clinic with the fragmented psyche of his patients, he is moved by the promise of the existence of a previous state where those parts belonged to a whole. In that movement, which presupposes a beginning and an asymptotic end (in the sense that it never encounters its parallel, which is its zero point), the possibility of an encounter with that structural loss and its enabling dimension begins to take place. In terms of language, for example, it is in the search of the immaculate child's voice that room is made for the previously mentioned translation, for the enrichment of language through that interlanguage, which is the voice that speaks from the fissures of the word. In that movement, a production of signifiers commences that manages to make that other, exiled in the language of the Other, speak. In the Name of the Other the apparition of a Proper Name begins to emerge.

The "what" and the "other"

The question then arises: What is that other?[1] But it seems we hide the answer from the start: what does that *what* veil, so much criticised by Heidegger (1955), who through Socrates makes its *premature* apparition in the history of thought? What else do we question with the *what*, if not the essence? Is it not precisely the essence that designates that by which something is just like itself, that by which a thing is not another, namely, the place of closure of the thing in a totality? If we enquire about the other *other*, we do not want to know what of the other is added in an absolute totality, but rather what is the radically other that appears there, prior to all *a priori*, looking at me full in the face, questioning me with its visage. In the introduction to *Totality and Infinity* (1961), Daniel E. Guillot (2006) affirms that:

> The other is precisely what cannot be neutralized in a conceptual content. The concept would place it at my disposal and it would thus suffer the violence of the conversion of the Other into Same. The idea of the infinite expresses this impossibility of finding a middle term—a concept—that can serve as buffer to the alterity of the Other. The latter as the absolute is a transcendence prior to all reason and to the universal, because it is, precisely, the source of all rationality and all universality. (p. 25)

Consequently, preceding all previousness, the other is at the same time unrepresentable and the source itself of the representational apparatus; it predates all foundation, but it is a foundation without *arche* of all ethics and all justice. Therefore, Levinas' statement according to which *ethics precedes ontology* gains meaning, since the *immemoriality* of the other for whom I have always been responsible (therein lies its relation with ethics) is previous and comes first before any ontology. Ethical reflection does not derive from ontology; the *other* has always been there, as a limit of all time and all thought.

In our time, the eye is undoubtedly the organ that most avoids the structural presence of castration. That point of fissure where the subject faints, where the field without borders of the impossible and the *non-totalising* is dethroned and defined, is ejected before the eye of technical reason, which sees everything or which, by its glance, makes a totality of what exists. But Johannes Angelus Silesius has already warned us- and not only him—in his *The Cherubinic Wanderer* (1675): "An eye that never deprives itself of the pleasure of seeing, finally blinds itself completely, and does not see itself" (without page). In that same movement of *observation-appropriation*, reason displaces itself from the place of the gaze and, becoming blind in that circularity where it frames what exists, pretends to be the optical referent of all that it is decreed through the refraction of light. That "bringing to light" as illumination of what *is*, as fluorescence of bodies starting from the concept, is silencing of the real insofar as presence of the alterity in what *there is* (*il y a*). But if this is the status of the gaze in the spectrum of the thinkable, then what is Levinas saying when he states that "ethics is an optics"? (1961, p. 23). Surely he does not highlight the optic that pretends to confine, with its gaze, the being to a representation, but an *a-representational* optics, prior to thought, that will allow the eye that is present there, vulnerable, waiting, to be affected by the face of the other. It is *of another mode of being*, that is, in the *beyond* of being.

But prior to all this, before the existence of an other different from me, before *me*, there is a radical *other* that challenges me. That absolute alterity does not circumscribe itself to my spoken word in my own language. It does not close itself in my conceptual totality, in the sense that my meaning entraps it, like that *meaning* that I can bestow on it; it is not the other of me, but the other *other*. That radical other does not fall into the framework of the confusion of tongues—the latter understood as the imposition of a language on another—but it preserves instead its place in the untouched of all translation, maintaining its difference; it is not spoken by others. Thus Ferenczian infancy meets with the Levinasian other (those two impossibles!), in that place preceding all *a priori*, before the decadence of desire and the birth of history. Locating all those places prior to all logical temporality of the structure, that is, of that place which lacks a *before*, they aim at rescuing the lost fundamental, but not for the sake of rebuilding metaphysics, since this would be death in act of difference and the singularity of childhood, but rather as a motor that mobilises, in one, the idea around ethics and, in the other, the direction of the cure in the analytic device. That radical difference, motive itself of its singularity as a *there is*, is the real that beckons, that seduces to murder, since maintaining the place of radical difference presents itself as an impossible; therefore, what is sought is to make of that *other* a representation, gathered within a same field of meaning, making of it a sameness, a totality. But that face of the radically different other articulates, at the same time, the phrase: "You shall not kill, do not make of me a representation, let me be from my singularity." This singularity is not its essence, as in Greek philosophy, nor its egoic fundamental in the modern sense, but above all *an-archy*, precisely without *arche*, without foundation. To affirm its essence would be to make of it, once again, sameness, totality; to be affected by its *an-archic* questioning is to preserve its place of radical alterity, of difference.

The displacement of the Other

To the figures of the orphan, the widow and the stranger, proposed by Levinas as places of the radical other, we should undoubtedly add at least one more: the displaced person. It is the face of the displaced that questions us at every corner, with other eyes, other worlds, and other skins. With his shield of pain, he passes through the spectre of difference. I kill him, I deprive him of his singularity, and I name him with my concept that makes of him a nothing, a vile difference from me. Thus there appears, in my violence, the face of evil, which is not one of guns and bombs that stripped him from his land, but that other more subtle violence, which, disguising itself as kindness and good intentions, becomes more dangerous because, *who cures the evil that good does?* As Lacan (1958) points out with respect to psychoanalytic technique:

> Kindness is undoubtedly more necessary here than anywhere else, but it couldn't cure the evil it engenders. The analyst who wants the good of the subject repeats that which he has learned in his training, including all its distortions. The most abhorrent education has never had another motive than the good of the subject. (My transl. p. 599)

Thus,

> evil is no longer a finitude which prevents the subject from elevating himself to the absolute, further than death, but the bad infinite of indetermination of the *there is*. It is not the void which surrounds being and which, ultimately, is an accomplice of being, but that nameless world of outer spaces and deserts which strives to reduce subjectivity to an inert element. (Guillot, 2006, p. 29)

And even so, despite this violence of kindness—this subliminal violence, which goes unnoticed in the cordiality of good intentions—an originating violence still exists, and emerges from all subjectivity; it is an essential violence, which is precisely that of the being who transcends all the thought that tries to grapple it into a whole; it is the violence of all that is infinite, its wonder.

But how does that otherness take place, how do I make experience of the other, of the infinite? Surely not with thought, if by thought we understand what Zenon did, that is, the other as One, *over here* from the multiple, since infinite is precisely that which overflows thought.

> The relation with infinity cannot, to be sure, be stated in terms of experience, for infinity overflows the thought that thinks it. Its very *infinition* is produced precisely in this overflowing. The relation with infinity will have to be stated in terms other than those of objective experience; but if experience precisely means a relation with the absolutely other, that is, with what always overflows thought, the relation with infinity accomplishes experience in the fullest sense of the word. (Levinas, 1961, p. 25)

Consequently, the infinite is not a representation, it is not the representation of the infinite but is, above all, that which escapes representation, fleeing from the concept.

Levinas breaks away from a tradition that places in sensibility the way in which intelligence apprehends the world with the information perceived through the senses. This only interests Levinas as a counterpoint of that other way sensibility has of disposing itself in opening to the other. The power of knowledge is no longer what governs the experience of sensibility as apprehension of the objects of the world and their transformation in phenomena, but of sensibility as sentiment.

The surface that exposes (and does not intervene) before the presence of the other is pure sentiment. Here a proximity with Benjamin appears with regard to experience that, regardless of the sensitive qualities or the mediation of thought, shakes the *ego* before the *extimity* of its being. The *pleasure* produced by sensibility without thought is the opening before the experience of the other, not as representation of the other *in* me, but as sensible alterity *before* me. What Levinas presents is not a dichotomy facing the ways of knowing the world, inscribed in a classic psychological tradition—and in philosophy, from where it originates—of perception/a-perception, sentiment/thought, affect/reason, but a way of *knowing* of the other, of what overflows the totality, without implying a *murder* of alterity as circumscription to a thought that makes of it sameness. It is the sensibility distanced from the *theory* of alterity, it is the sensibility before the infinite beyond the *concept* of infinite, it is difference beyond the *discourse* of difference. Sensibility as a tool of knowledge builds walls across the other; sensibility, as vulnerability before the other who beckons, is an opening to the face of the other.

That opening to the other does not part from an intentionality that wants to allow alterity to participate. That would be returning to the egoism that closes the opening in concentric circles, the *pleasure* of *me in me*. It is precisely the passivity of *letting* oneself be affected by the other, without that *letting* becoming an activity, what leads to the other calling upon me. I do not decide it, it is prior to me, it has always been there. It does not appear as a theme for representation. In this regard, subjectivity appears as this having always *been offered* to the other. It is precisely here that it is possible to enounce once again Levinas' phrase according to which *ethics precedes ontology*. Ferenczi's emphasis on sympathy in his clinical practice is also worth remembering. According to what he stated in his *Clinical Diary* (1932b), the analyst's sympathy as an essential element of psychoanalytical work implies finding a means whereby that *other* who lies on the couch—that child lost in signifiers of the Other, in the hypnosis of that word of the Other—can appear; making myself sensible to that other, and, in that *letting myself be affected*, approaching the shipwrecked childhood.

The other and language: a pro-vocative proposal

But what is the other *other* if not the other of me? It is not what I am not, my *not-I*, what exceeds my frontier, demarcating an inside and an outside. It is not even the other of me at the point at which I fade away, there where the ego sleeps, moves away, in the gaze that the mirror gives back and that I do not recognise as mine, that foreignness with one's own being of Rimbaud's famous "Car Je est un autre".[2] Neither is it the other of the depths and surfaces, motor of the lapsus, the joke, and oneiric productions, reservoir of childhood desires. Neither is it the I that finds itself identical even in its alterations and which becomes terrified before the alterity of what it is. Neither is it another child who awaits in the folds of language and who desires in my desire. Levinas (1961) tells us:

> The other metaphysically desired is not "other" like the bread
> I eat, the land in which I dwell, the landscape I contemplate, like,
> sometimes, myself to myself, this "I" this "other." I can "feed" on
> these realities and, to a very great extent, satisfy myself, as though
> I had simply been lacking them. Their *alterity* is thereby reabsorbed
> into my own identity as a thinker or a possessor. The metaphysical
> desire tends towards *something else entirely*, toward the *absolutely
> other*. (p. 33, italics in original)

But, what of the difference when I enquire about the *what* of the other? That which structurally vitiates language overcomes desire inasmuch as it is metaphysical. Can the question about the *what* make room for the *completely other*, to the *absolutely other*, or is language, from the start, sameness? Is the question about the *what* of the other so untenable in itself, as a semantic articulation, like a ball of sand thrown into the sea? Is language necessarily a damned field for reflection about the other? Can we know about the *other* from an articulation of signifiers or is the beckoning of the other's face necessarily *asignifying*? And even so, Levinas tells us that language is a terrain where the relation of the Same and the Other takes place. That relationship, which is metaphysics itself, absolves Sameness and the Other from the sum; it is the *exit from itself* of sameness. In Levinas' word, it is *Religion*.

Given this situation, the question necessarily arises regarding the status of that metaphysics to which Levinas "returns". In that struggle spearheaded by Nietzsche with his "philosophy of the hammer", which continues in Heidegger's *Destruktion* and which accompanies the bulk of contemporary philosophy—all for the sake of overthrowing metaphysics, turning back towards the *logos*, re-establishing non-metaphysical thought, unsupported by transcendental principles—, Levinas makes his entrance, introducing concepts such as *metaphysical Desire* and *Religion*, to think about the relationship of the Other and the Same.

What place can we give to this thought that can escape the danger that always comes hand in hand with the resurrection of old idols? Why include, once again, under the wing of philosophic reflection and in the current task of thought, these notions and these terms, so awkward in our century, as elements that in themselves ruin all possibility of producing new thought? We have already brought up this issue in relation to Ferenczi: how can we think about the tender figure of childhood in his work without implying overturning the Freudian discovery of the child as a desiring, instinctual, perverse polymorphous? Just as we have proceeded with Ferenczi, so shall we with Levinas. To do justice to his way of inserting those concepts into his philosophical work, it is necessary to understand Levinasian metaphysics from the point of view of the precepts of his own thought; a metaphysics that returns, perhaps, but not as cephalous matter carved in the empty place left by the death of God, because it is a rupture with a tradition of thought that, based on the *what* and on reason's way of conducting itself, negates difference and what is to come in the manifold of sense. Heidegger (1955) criticises this thought in his way of asking about the *what* of things, in asking about truth as sufficiency of the same, for its *ipseity* and, in Levinas' terms (1961), the manifestation of its "egology" (p. 44). Levinas' thinking, in this sense, is not necessarily a "religious turn", opposed to *anti-philosophy*, according to Alemán (2000), the latter understood as placing philosophy on the road towards an *other thinking*. Neither is it the return to the philosophy of the Enlightenment, because that unconditioned is neither a representation nor an essence, but a way in which the advent to the real is incited. Levinas is conscious of the dangers that the resurrection of sleeping gods can bring. If he advocates an ethical principle *prior to everything a priori* it is because the latter is not a foundation but above all *an-archy*. It is not a foundation to the way in which one is brought to the presence of sameness. It is, above all, an *immemorial past*, which does not come to meet us, and of which I have nevertheless always made myself responsible. It is not *immemorial* because of a weakness of memory but because of the *insurmountable impossibility of time*, it is the *other* as threshold of thought. It is the *first of all*, prior to any effect of representation. This way of understanding the *immemorial* in Levinas serves as a bridge that returns us to what we have defined as *structural* with respect to child-hood in Ferenczi: the place of what is lost, absent, evanescent, impossible, inevitable; the place of need.

Returning to our thoughts regarding language: if language is the material that makes up thought and, in turn, tends to make of the multiple *One* and sameness, how is it that in the experience of language I make a place for the other? Here Levinas refers to a fundamental distinction in order to understand how opening to alterity proceeds in the experience of the word, which is the difference between *saying* and *what is said* and the participation of the *vocative* in that experience. If the other calls upon me, a way must be found to respond to that other, not with my *word-appropriation* but with the *saying-opening*.

> Saying approaches the other by breaking through the noema involved in intentionality, turning inside out, "like a cloak," consciousness which, by itself, would have remained for-itself even in its intentional aims [...] The subject in saying approaches a neighbor in expressing itself, in being expelled, in the literal sense of the term, out of any locus, no longer *dwelling*, not stomping any ground. Saying uncovers, beyond nudity, what dissimulation there may be under the exposedness of a skin laid bare. (Levinas, 1974, pp. 48–49, italics in original)

Levinas finds the relationship with the *vocative* not only in the adoption of French, but also in the surviving presence of his native tongue, Lithuanian. Thus, it is the other who is alluded to in the enunciation of the words—not in what is enounced—, without an *other* being subject or object.

Language in this regard is produced by the beckoning of the other, allowing me to speak. Nevertheless, in its double edge, language is also a way of silencing the other, depriving him of his alterity and surrendering before the threat of destroying his difference with my conceptual encompassing. One's own voice is not the voice that the ego uses to speak, but the voice with which the real of singularity manifests itself. The mother tongue is always—and from the start—a foreign tongue, but it is also something more. As the Colombian writer Mario Flórez affirms, the mother tongue is not "the language with which one learned to speak, but the language with which one learned to be silent" (quoted by Ospina, 2007, p. 68). At this point the forms articulated by

Ferenczi and Levinas find their perfect circle, since the confusion of tongues is not the result of what the adult tells the child, of the content of what is said, but is solely due to the fact of speaking. This difference, which provides a structural viewpoint, and not a psychological one, to Ferenczian thought, reveals once again the paradox of the confusion of tongues. The position of the subject that speaks is always traumatic: it supposes being in the profound sleep of the Other's meaning (that the Other gives). But the awakening from that sleep does not imply an illumination, in the style of the mystics where an Adamic relationship with objects and the adoption of a language that entails no babelisation whatsoever, is recovered. On the contrary, *the awakening is an awakening to the confusion of tongues*; it occurs in the very rupture of language, through the analytical relationship, through the enrichment produced by the interlanguage (*Zwischensprache*): the sole language in which it is possible for desire to speak.

In Spanish, *vocative* is a synonym of *remarkable*, that is, it allows us to understand that what is at stake is the call of the other, the ear readied to his difference, my body lent to his caress. In speaking, "the *one* is exposed to the *other* as a skin is exposed to that which hurts it" (Levinas, 1975, p. 102). It is passivity with respect to that wound, the offering of the skin for the caress and the bruise. But even if one enters the game of significations and signifiers, it is above all signification prior to any objectivisation. The other as *vocative*, as a *call* to which I respond, is not the object, nor even the subject of my enunciations; that is, without appropriation: *speech* in the aperture of being. Only in this "Here I am" of language is it possible that it will be able to express the *other insofar as other*. In the disposition of this *charity* towards the other, even if betraying language itself, the word can avoid erasing the other, its vanishing place, my appropriation.

Another dimension of language is thus opened, a *beyond* of the traditional language of philosophy, to demarcate its object. Levinas (1951) says that

> It is not on behalf of a divorce between philosophy and reason that we hold to a judicious language. All the same we are entitled to ask whether reason, presented as the possibility of such a language, does in fact necessarily precede it, or if language is not rather founded on a relation anterior to comprehension and constituting reason? (p. 123)

This *prior to* that Levinas alludes to, as foundation and melting of language, is precisely the presence of that other in the immemorial past; it is from there that all words and all ethical reflection depart. Levinas appeals to what, from Ferenczi, we have termed the language of tenderness, the lost childhood, the child free from loss. He wants his ethical reflection to depart from here. It is subsequent to the other that the word becomes custodian of the *quidity*, and the alterity of the other sacrifices itself to maintain the one-ness of the existent. But for Levinas the possibility that all language will not necessarily be confusion of tongues is given by that *prior to*, by that beckoning of the other, which is heard and speaks before the representation I make of its voice or with what its voice tells me. But, in this sense, Levinas appeals only to the most traumatising dimension of the confusion of tongues: the one that only permits the same to speak and the other to hide itself within the folds of the signifiers. It is in the preservation of that primordial space that a place extends itself for Levinas so that the response to the other will not be wiped off the map of difference, making of it the object of my understanding, a victim of my tool of knowledge. We would distance ourselves from Levinas if we tried to abolish all possible dimension to the confusion of tongues, if we searched for a language free from desire and free from the hearsay of the Other.

What other other

Levinas is interested in a subjectivity that will not be just a protest against the totality, but that will above all be singularity founded in the idea of the infinite. The latter does not find its place in the opposition to the finite, it is not its counterface, but, insofar as being radically outside of all totality and as founding place of what *is*, prior to all foundation. Metaphysical desire does not operate like a desire at fault that searches for its object to fulfil and complete itself, that desire for the *lack of being* highlighted by Lacan (1960–61) in his lecture on Plato's "The banquet"; instead, it desires beyond that which satisfies it. Metaphysical desire, therefore, wishes for the absolutely other, beyond the bread that satisfies hunger, the bed that removes tiredness, and the water that quenches thirst; it is the *metaphysical* that, as tendency of desire, does not close itself in a totality with the other. Only in this way can the *same* know of the *other* without depriving it, in that knowledge, of its alterity. That

radical Other—that is, my vulnerability, my passivity—does not enu-
merate itself with me, because it would be enumeration of the *One*, loss
of liberty and, therefore, sameness.

There appears, then, a demand for the production of a new routing
and processing of thought in order to respond to the other—not conceptually, representationally—who calls upon us with his face, from his
radical alterity. That new way in which thought disposes itself, and the
task of philosophy, is what Derrida (1995b) evokes through the words
of Blanchot on the day of farewell, *a-Dieu*, of the Lithuanian philosopher: "It is as though there were here a new departure in philosophy
and a leap that it, and we ourselves, were urged to accomplish" (p. 9).
It is not only Levinas who beckons us with his words, or through the
words evoked by others, by Blanchot, by Derrida, or by the philosophical output of France at the end of the twentieth century; it is the *other*
who calls upon us through their writings, which work like a magnifying glass, microscope to the other, and which—without putting definite concepts ahead but instead an infinite succession of sprains that
try to deprive the space which the *Same* robs from the *Other*—manages
to remove the representational veil, the familiar face, so that, regardless of the features, the eyes might appear; the circumspect rictus, the
unchanging and inappropriable face of the other who is there prior to
us, before us, prior to everything *a priori*, prior to me and before me. But
this removing of the veil is not a disclosure only understood as *aletheia*,
that is, as an apparition of the other in the spectrum of the thinkable, but
as the way in which the infinite makes its entrance into language without *making itself seen*. Thus the Levinasian reflection regarding the question "*what* other *other?*" can be enounced: it does not appear in thinking
the different—even if that reflection resorts to the world from its edges,
from the fringes that demarcate an inside and an outside—but in being
exposed to the other. In this way—even though at the borders the eye
is sharpened and the optics that denounce the totality as enemy of difference are carried out—it is in the exposure to the other that the ear
sharpens and it becomes possible to hear the knuckles of that other, of
that alterity that knocks at my door. And if I manage to hear them and
open the door it is not so that the other may enter my dwelling and my
refuge, becoming *my* tenant or *my* guest, but to maintain that door open
and closed at the same time, so that it will not only be the other who
enters, but me who goes out, not only from the comfort of my dwelling

but from the comfort of my being. It is in the *departure from being* that the other's beckoning, the unrest before the other, the epiphany of the other's face, is made possible.

Awakening the other

Ferenczi also wished that other to knock at his door, procuring this through his technical innovations. In the invocation of that other, he sought for an awakening. Lacan, according to J.-A. Miller (1986), tried to do the same with his short sessions: to produce a discomfort in his analysands that would lead to that anti-natural desire of awakening from their various dreams, including the analytic dream. Awakening is related to the desire of an encounter with the real, which nevertheless is an impossibility from the start. Awakening is pierced by the same paradoxical impossibility that the confusion of tongues implies: there is no "beyond" of the confusion of tongues further than the *desire* for a "beyond" of the confusion of tongues. In the same way that poets aim at a "beyond" of language by means of language itself, exploiting the senses, producing language effects, but through the word, psychoanalysis aims at a "beyond" of the confusion of tongues that will rescue that which enables the confusion of tongues itself, it aims at producing the desire for an awakening to the real even if meeting that real is impossible. If it is not possible, and this also applies to the *other* in Levinas and to the *child* in Ferenczi, why aim at it? Because it is in that movement, in that infinite, in that promise of encounter and of arrival, that the *other* makes its appearance: the vestiges of that subject, strewn in the language of the Other, appear, manifest in the desire of the analyst, which is none other than the desire to produce an awakening.

Here we can clarify something that is articulated throughout the issue we are discussing: just as there is no beyond of the confusion of tongues, neither is there an awakening to the real. In what has been proposed up to now, a series of polarities would appear which are actually movements over the same Möbius strip: *Ursprache*—language of communication (language of concepts), language of tenderness—language of passion, childhood—adulthood, sleep—awakening. Precisely between those poles lies the work of the analyst who, availing himself of that *intermediate, daimonic tongue*, aims at making possible the always ruined encounter that occurs between sleep and awakening.

CHAPTER ELEVEN

Lacan. On the verges of psychoanalytic experience

Having introduced Levinasian and Benjaminian reflection regarding language, the question necessarily arises: How can we incorporate this *other* in psychoanalysis? How can we prompt its emergence, its manifestation, within the analytic sessions? What can be done so that psychoanalytical technique may be an opening towards difference, towards radical alterity, and not a tool of sameness? We should ask ourselves, therefore, if the possibility of that opening exists from the start or if, on the contrary, it is a logical border impossible to break down.

As mentioned at the beginning of this study, Ferenczi aims at the discovery of a real characteristic of language. Psychoanalysis, as a technique of speech, is pierced in turn by the limits of language. The proposition of thinkers such as Levinas and Benjamin is to examine up to what point language vitiates all reflection outside the metaphysical categories and prevents what, since Heidegger, has been referred to as *a road towards another way of thinking*.

That *appropriative* way language has, its tendency to sameness, its violence as a way of imposing the word over another, is what, from Ferenczi onwards, we have termed the "confusion of tongues". Benjamin, on the other hand, proposes translation as a way, if not of circumventing, at least of *making with* the confusion of tongues, which will manage to express the meanings of language, renovating it permanently, not as a tendency towards the sameness that implies loyalty of the translation to its original, but rather as a new text, with innovative meanings, bearing its own uniqueness. The translator lends himself to the task of approaching language in this way; at this point it is worth considering the relationship between the figure of the translator in Benjamin and the psychoanalyst within analytical practice.

Levinas, for his part, constructs a work that is a way around thought proposed as an opening to the other, as a way of opening that space to the other, despite the constraints of language. Levinas, with the care of his word, disposes of language in such a way that he speaks of nothing else apart from the other, but without ever naming it in the classic sense in which language names things, because he knows that, in that same movement, he ends up making of the *other* the *same*. He manages, however, within the possibilities offered by the word, to point out the issue that language brings with it, so tainted by metaphysics, together with the way in which philosophy has thought the other and, thus, draws an outline that allows the presence of that other *other*. The opening offered by a return beyond language allows sensibility before the other, becoming sensitive to the other.

As J.-A. Miller (1986) points out with respect to the limits of language in relation to psychoanalytic practice, "the signifier 'one' has a sedative virtue. The primary fact of all discourse is to lull, and this also applies to the analyst when he abandons himself to the task of listening to his patient, to reversed hypnosis" (p. 118). However, from where should one proceed to incorporate this philosophical thought within psychoanalysis? What bridges can we count on to open up those transferences? Undoubtedly, the open ground into which this this reflection can be introduced is the work and thought of the French psychoanalyst Jacques Lacan and particularly his developments with regard to the concept of *the real*, a concept used in different ways and at different moments in his oeuvre, and which must be defined.

Although not generally agreed upon as a specific definition of the real, it is clear that in what has been referred to as "his last teaching", Lacan is developing, more profoundly, what the real is. In those last seminars, Lacan highlights the more obscure and complex nuances of his concept of the real, undertaking his most sophisticated experiments in order to introduce that real as an issue within psychoanalytic practice. That is why Alemán (2006) is correct when he suggests that Lacan's last teaching is not really psychoanalysis, that it should perhaps go under another name since, if the history of psychoanalysis has been the confusion of tongues from the start, this last period of Lacan's work is an opening to circumvent—or confront—that confusion. By incorporating elements unrelated to psychoanalysis, from exteriority, Lacan proceeds to open up possible ways of avoiding the complexity implied in thinking from outside the very limits of language. The philosophers, psychoanalysts, and poets who have considered this issue, and have interacted throughout our study, probably come together at this juncture.

Ferenczi, on the other hand, met with countless unsuccessful attempts at incorporating that real into analytic practice, trying to keep it in its place without removing it from the scene. He considered that the way to include it was through those technical variations already alluded to: active technique, relaxation and neo-catharsis, and mutual analysis. His interest in the body lay in the fact that he found in it a ground free of the contamination of language, bearer of the most profound and essential havoc of trauma. His passion for the archaic, so daring and poetically rendered in *Thalassa: A Theory of Genitality* (1924a), is probably an attempt to find the place, prior to the semantic ordination of the bodies, that operates through language acquisition. The archaic in Ferenczi is that ground similar to Benjamin's childhood, that area prior to the confusion of tongues where hope for a true cure awaits. Ferenczi himself did not remain free from that confusion: the illness that led to his death, a pernicious anaemia, was, for him, the persistence of the un-analysed nucleus that had always dwelt in the folds of his soma, fueled by his late disagreements with Freud, awaiting there like an unborn son, ancient and silent.

Consequently, making this counterpoint between Ferenczi and Lacan, and suggesting that Ferenczi came up against the real that has been named "confusion of tongues"—and which he wanted to insert into psychoanalytical practice but was unable to do so, due to his method of introducing variables into the technique—it will be necessary to review how Lacan proceeds and what remains of his work that will allow us to continue thinking about that opening *to make with* the limits of language in psychoanalysis. In order to demarcate what he articulates as real in his last teachings it will be necessary to refer specifically to some issues with respect to Lacan's relationship with philosophy.

Lacan and antiphilosophy

Through (the unfortunately named) antiphilosophy, Alemán (1999) sets out to think about the relationship between Lacan and philosophers and his particular way of incorporating philosophical reflection into psychoanalysis. The term antiphilosophy was not invented by Alemán; he adopts it from words pronounced by Lacan himself in 1974 (Lacan, 1975). Alemán states that "antiphilosophy is not a specialty, just as there shouldn't be a specialty in topology or linguistics, but rather it's one of the various ways of speaking about what the analytic experience consist of, and it's also a discussion about its way of transmitting it" (p. 28). Thus, as a way of referring to analytical experience, antiphilosophy does not make its entrance with Lacan but with Freud himself, who, despite wishing to be modern and brilliant, ended up coming up against the ruptures of modernity and the cracks that revealed the inconsistency of his project. Such was the Freudian discovery of the porosity of modernity. When the horrors of the Second World War became more than evident, even to those who had deafened their ears and had refused to listen to the warnings—warnings that had appeared since the romantic movements, with *Sturm und Drang* and the damned poets, and later with the Primitivists and other counterculture movements of the twentieth century, and, finally psychoanalysis—the fall of the Project of Modernity became inevitable; the logic according to which instrumental reason would lead to progress and to the realisation of the species bore beneath its wings a diabolical project, and the thinkers who emerged from the holocaust had no choice other than to refer to Freudian thought in order to unravel some truth from the logic of horror that definitely vitiated all previous thought. Freud's discoveries regarding trauma and repetition compulsion now made that "metaphysics of emancipation", which had raised the flag of modernity, totally despicable.

Freud thus emerges, according to Eugenio Trías' terminology, as a bearer of "reason at the frontier", who dismantles the inconsistency of the modern project and unveils—in Möbian fashion—how the horror of the twentieth century is a logical consequence of the modern project itself and not of its failure. In this way, paraphrasing Freud and inverting the equation, *the modern project triumphs precisely where it fails*; the horrors and disappointments of the war, the infinite number of deaths,

Auschwitz and Treblinka, the 5000 degrees at which human bodies burned in Hiroshima and Nagasaki, are the realisation and triumph of the logic that governed the project of modernity.

Freud introduces instinct in a way that has never been done in the history of thought. He places there that which appears to him, rather than it having been sought out, and in spite of his own modern appetite, which is what Alemán (1999), with genius, describes as "a hinge between the field of sense and the field of drives" (p. 31). That "hinge" established by Freudian thought, rather than being the abyss of its inconsistency, is the epicentre of its tremor and its power. Where the opponents of psychoanalysis indicate the lack of epistemological consistency in Freud's thinking, psychoanalysts recognise its power. Why is Freud's reason referred to as "reason at the frontier"? Precisely because by placing reflection on that hinge, he lays out the place of *extimity* that unites and separates at the same time. And what is it that unites and separates simultaneously? Nothing less than sense and drive. Here we are once again at the very limit of analytic practice, before that real, before that apparently unbreakable point of the confusion of tongues. Because precisely what that limit indicates is up to what point—or at which point—sense touches the body, that soma "beyond" the caress of the symbolic.

This Freudian discovery, which places thought at the limit between sense and drive, does not occur systematically in the way that science exploits reason. "It's not a matter of founding the scientific nature of psychoanalysis according to epistemologies; on the contrary, if psychoanalysis cannot be a science, it is not due to a shortfall, but because it deals with that which science excludes in order to establish itself as such" (Alemán, 1999, p. 33).[1] That is, the beyond of instrumental reason, the analytical magnifying glass, that reveals its ruptures, enjoys at the same time an internal logic, which is necessary in order to trace and elucidate its own boundaries, with the ultimate goal of understanding how it proceeds and how it functions, and thus, unravels. And it is possible to advance the certainty that that which science excludes is nothing less than the real, that which, outside of the symbolic, permanently calls upon all order of reality. Nevertheless, not for this reason does psychoanalysis run through a beyond of logic. Lacan worries about finding ways of intervening at the boundary between sense and enjoyment, and sense and the real, in order to find a way in which, from sense, it is possible to intervene upon the real. If we have maintained that Ferenczi's work operates as an attempt to articulate the real that his clinical skill reveals to him, it must be seen as to whether Lacan's work regarding this topic will offer the tools for a knowledge regarding that real in psychoanalysis.

Lacan highlights various premises of Heidegger's thinking, among them the way in which each period, as if brought from being to the presence, is at the same time the way in which that being is veiled. Therefore, the way of being of *being* in each epoch is none other than under the guise of concealment. That concealment of being, suffered by philosophy, its confusion of being and the entity, is read by Lacan's psychoanalytical mind through the mechanisms of repression and foreclosure. Previously, we pointed out that the way in which Ferenczi returns to the psychoanalytic scene is through the return of the repressed and that, with every new appearance—each new book, lecture, or article, whether about his work or his person, confused so many times—emerges the new form that veils him, hiding the real that assisted as awakening in that new work. Heidegger, therefore, aims at an awakening of philosophy that lies in the dream of the *entity*, a dream whose guardian is metaphysics itself. Lacan finds that post-Freudian psychoanalysts are the most *philosophical* in the sense that they find themselves in the oneiric depths of metaphysics and, worse still, they are not in the least bit aware that that is the dream they dream. This goes hand in hand with what Žižek points out in several of his writings and lectures about ideologies: *one does not know that one knows*, in the sense that all orders of thought are operated upon, without the subject knowing that this lies behind his analyses, decisions, and conclusions.

With regard to Heidegger's work, Alemán (2000) affirms that

> we know that the project "Being and Time" is abandoned for lack of a language, of a relationship between the thinker and the language that will allow him to continue with his task. Heidegger abandons his project because that moment arrives when language already disposes of such a semantic load, such metaphysical inertia, that it makes it unsuitable for producing that crossing of philosophy which he has demanded for a long time. (p. 114)

We also know that Rimbaud abandoned his literary project: after exploiting the phonemes and signifiers of the French language, he abandons himself in the forests of Albania to smuggle merchandise, arms, and, as some authors have suggested, slaves. Language was not sufficient for him either. And undoubtedly, it is true that with language the real cannot be expressed; it is logically impossible. However, it is also true that the machinery of language can be put at the service of silencing the real and this is not what the thought here expressed wishes. "If the real is excluded from the field of meaning, with what footprints can it be eventually read" (Alemán, 2006, p. 18). The finger cannot touch the hole but it can touch the edges; in the same way, language can operate as pressure on the lateral and the surrounding skin of the wound in order to open it, dilate it, and, in this way, listen to what speaks within it. Thus, we are not before the *nominative* function of language as silence of the real, nor before the concrete/abstract language of Lévi-Strauss, but before a *dilative* function of language that expands the semantic pores of the word in such a way that the real breathes and airs itself out, its *pneuma* rising to the surface and "letting itself be seen".

With the artifice of *antiphilosophy*, Alemán (2000) manages to focus on the topic at the central point of this investigation, namely: is an analysis that produces an awakening to the confusion of tongues possible? Alemán suggests that:

> The problem of whether psychoanalysis addresses the real or not is an issue which Lacan made explicit, but which can be found, of course, in Freud. Two options arise: either psychoanalysis is no more than the permanent commentary, inexhaustible and lucid, of an impasse, or it touches something of the real. (p. 42)

This could be enounced in another way: is psychoanalysis pure dream, pure auto-erotic satisfaction of the drive to sleep, or is it also the possibility of an awakening? Freud will ask himself this question when he considers the effects of analytical therapy in his traumatised patients beyond the confines of transference. Ferenczi will also ask himself this question when he examines in his *Clinical Diary* (1932b) at which point it is possible to maintain that apparent unity of parts of his psychotic patients beyond the walls of his consulting room so that they will not succumb to the collapse caused by the brutality of the *splitting* (Gutiérrez-Peláez, 2006). Thus, what is interesting about Lacan's thought is that it does not end at the point of thinking the real as that which, together with the symbolic, excludes itself, but rather as the place of frontier, of coastline, and overlap. What the composition of the Borromean knot immediately reveals is that the Imaginary, the Symbolic, and the Real do not adjoin but overlap.

Lacan and the openness to the real

Slavoj Žižek, in a lecture given at the Psychoanalytical Association of Buenos Aires (APdeBA) in 2004 differentiates three types of real, which, more than three different and distinctive entities, are three modes of one same real; interlinked registers that mutually affect each other. Žižek sets them out as follows:

> There are three modalities of the Real: the "real Real" (the horrifying thing, the primordial object, from Irma's throat up to the *Alien*), the "symbolic Real" (the Real as consistency: the signifier reduced to a senseless formula, like the quantitative physics formulae which we cannot translate to the daily experience of our universe of meaning) and the "imaginary Real" (the mysterious *je ne sais quoi*, the unfathomable "something" by which the sublime dimension shines through a common object). Thus, the Real is indeed these three dimensions at the same time: the abysmal maelstrom which destroys any consistent structure; the mathematic consistent structure of reality; and the pure and fragile appearance. (2004)

For Žižek, the real will not be the last dimension of the traumatic, its final evidence, but that traumatic Thing, *Das Ding*, is, instead, nothing less than the veil of horror that underlies it, the notion itself of the real as an unbearable thing. For the Slovenian philosopher, there is an even more radical version of the real. Using the metaphor of Einstein's notions of curved space, and understanding with them that it is not matter that curves space but curved space that produces matter, he affirms that trauma continues to be a masquerade and that the real is a product of the inconsistencies of reality. Similarly, with respect to the alterations in the perception of reality, they do not occur due to the insistence of the real over the hegemony of the sense organs; instead, perceptive alteration is the very evidence of the real.

Thus, Žižek reads the different spheres of the Borromean knot—the Symbolic, the Imaginary, and the Real—as interdependent, each one affecting the others. His concept could be represented as follows:

	Real	*Symbolic*	*Imaginary*
Real	The horrible thing	The formula without meaning	The real of illusion
Symbolic	The formula without meaning	Speech as such, speech that signifies	Symbols and archetypes (Jungian)
Imaginary	The real of illusion	Symbols and archetypes (Jungian)	The image as such, seductive

Žižek, supported by the writings of Jonathan Lear, suggests that the same criticism that Hegel made about Kant, could be applied to Freud; namely, that before the discovery of a negativity, he proposed a positivity. Hegel criticises the fact that, upon discovery of the inconsistency of the cognition of reality, Kant formulates the *thing-in-itself* as positivity that restores the order of things, even if that order can be the foundation of a disorder resulting in chaos.

Freud, faced with the evidence of trauma and the intricate way in which it occurs along with repetition, proposes drive dualism, that is, the life drive and the death drive as explicative positivities to account for the gap that appears in the notion of trauma. Thus, for Žižek, following Lear, the *death drive* is not the name of unbearable trauma but the veil laid before it, before its evidence, before its unfathomable gap. The real, therefore, is not the inaccessible Thing, but the distance itself located in the meantime, which makes the access to the Thing impossible. Thus, in his relationship with truth, Žižek appears in a dimension that is neither Kant's nor Nietzsche's: truth is not the thing in itself, but it is not pure relativity either, because there is a truth that is not relative; namely, the truth of the gap that asserts itself as impossibility of all neutrality and all ultimate truth. The impossibility of knowledge without distortion is not the result of the immanence of the real, but the *de facto* evidence of the trauma of the real. Trauma is the footprint of the real, not its product.

To a certain extent, trauma opposes itself to the symbolic because "by definition, trauma is something which cannot be remembered; integrating it to its symbolic narrative, in such a way that it repeats itself indefinitely, and returns to harass the subject" (Žižek, 2004). The real Real, which is the Real in its most extreme dimension, is the evidence of the most archaic trauma, pure negativity, and constitutively incapable of symbolically processing itself. Therefore, all elaboration around the real is, from the start, a veil to the real, a screen placed before the horror that lies underneath. It is possible to affirm, in general, that the relationship with the real is always affected by the entrance into language. The real functions as an impossible in the sense that it cannot express itself through language because the entrance into language itself is an irrevocable separation from the real. But this does not mean that the influence of the real ceases. It is the wall that awaits in language and in fantasies. Such is the double purpose of trauma: on the one hand, the entrance into language is traumatic because it alters a way of relating with the world and imprints the gap in the real, and, on the other, the imminent presence of the real in the withdrawal of the symbolic is experienced as a flood of anxiety, which is the very footprint of trauma.

It is necessary to pin down this notion of the real as *the gap itself* in relation to Lacan's seminars, in order to see in what context it is possible to rely on such a statement. The concept of the real in Lacan undergoes several changes and mutations. We observe how in his early writings and seminars the notion of the "real" is so much closer to that of "reality" and its imaginary dimension. It is worth remembering, for example, the treatment he gives to the real in his "Schema R" in "A preliminary question to all possible treatment of psychosis" (1957–58).

In Lacan's Seminar II, *The Ego in Freud's Theory* (1954), for example, the real appears as that which lacks fissures. In the analysis that he makes of Freud's text, "Instincts and their vicissitudes" (1915c), Lacan affirms that the real cannot be conceived in relation to an interiority and an exteriority, precisely due to the absence of fissures proper to it. There appears, thus, a first dimension of the real as unknowable unless through the symbolic register. Nevertheless, at this moment, Lacan still thinks of the "real" as "reality" and designates it as the place of what is unknowable of reality itself. It is in relation to an imaginary and a symbolic that some framework of reality may appear. It is not until Book VI, *Desire and Its Interpretation* (1959), that the notion of the real acquires a forceful twist. There Lacan outlines a clear difference between reality and the real:

> That is to say that the *a*, the object of desire, in its nature is a residue, a remainder. It is the residue left by the being to which the speaking subject is confronted to, in any possible demand. And this is why the object rejoins the real. This is how it participates in it. I am saying the real, and not reality because reality is constituted by all the halters that human symbolism, in a more or less perspicacious fashion, passes through the neck of the real in so far as it makes of them the objects of its experience. (1959, Class 27, 1 July)

The real, in its relation with the object *a*, appears as the dimension of greatest link to trauma and, therefore, to repetition. Consequently, Lacan can enounce that the real presents itself precisely in *that which always returns to the same place*. That which returns through time and which assures itself in its persistence is what articulates all possible theory around an assembling of reality.

We could suggest as a last clear definition of the real provided by Lacan the one that appears in "Television" (1970) according to which *the impossible is the Real*, that is, impossible insofar as it cannot be written.[2] This statement had already appeared before in Lacan's thought, at least since his Seminar XI, *The Four Fundamental Concepts of Psychoanalysis* (1964), where he affirms that

> [t]his function of the impossible must be dealt with prudence, as all function which presents itself in a negative manner. I would simply like to suggest that the best way of dealing with these notions is not taking them by their negation. This method would take us to the question of the possible, and the impossible is not necessarily the opposite of the possible or, since the opposite of the possible is the real, we must define the real as the impossible. (1964, Class 13, 6 May)

But once again Žižek will give a twist to this statement, which in our view does justice to what Lacan affirms. The real is not impossible in the sense that it is something that will never happen; the real does happen, but as an always failed encounter, and precisely that questioning of the real is what operates as traumatic. The difficulty is that, precisely where we think the real may be found, what we really encounter is the illusion, the mirage that, dressed up as real, continues to hide what is truly traumatic. For Žižek, the presence of the real is not given by the distance that the object may have in relation to the Thing, that distance where all apprehension of a true encounter beyond the perceptive phenomenon is vetoed, but the gap lies rather in the object itself; it is the latter that is split, broken. That inevitable gap present in the object itself is its place of splitting. Therefore, rather than the real being impossible, what is real is impossibility itself. The encounter with the real is a failed encounter, one that is not produced but which has effects, and one of them undoubtedly is trauma: trauma as an effect of the real. There, that dimension of the real is woven, which is nothing less than a new veil laid before the real.

When we affirm that what confronts the clinical practitioner nowadays is the real, what are we trying to say? That the clinical object itself is beyond the possibilities of clinical practice, in the real that is beyond the field of influence of the practice, operating in the subject ine a dimension from which an encounter will never be possible? Or that what the patient brings to the sessions is an absence of masquerade, such a phantasmatic failure that he is prevented from building a scene that will allow him to process some of the anxiety that invades him; and for this reason, what appears as symptomatic is precisely the lack of (symbolic) symptoms, namely, a pure invasion of anxiety (a-objectal) that evinces a horrifying proximity with the real? Or is that immanence of the real also a veil that is laid there, either by the patient or the analyst himself, when placing the real as a place of the impossible, as a veil before the trauma of a possible encounter with the real? Ultimately, is the clinical reading of the relationship with the real also a veil that excludes that more radical real, its absolute *otherness*, and a way of circumscribing it, as far as impossibility, as possibility within the field of *sameness* of clinical practice?

CHAPTER TWELVE

Awakening to trauma: writings on traumatophilia

*Anxiety hysterias and conversion hysterias
in the spectrum of war pathologies*

Agamben (1999) refers to a poem by Primo Levi, which speaks of the uncertainty of the survivors of the concentration camps, and whether their actual lives are a dream or an awakening: "Now we have found our homes again; our bellies are full; we have finished telling our tales. It's time. Soon we will once again hear the foreign order: *Wstawac*" (quoted by Agamben, 1999, p. 102). That foreign word, *Wstawac* (waking up), appears in place of the Name, that is, of that which has no name: the horror vis-à-vis the awakening, the last word that beckons from the *real*; the occurrence of the impossible. For the victims of the concentration camps, many are the processes that converge and which they experience, such as the loss of temporality, of spatiality, of humanity, but there is one that presents itself with more violence: the witnessing of their own desubjectivation—paradoxically, because, even though from a place of torture, of degradation and deprivation, it exposes that which produces subjectivity itself: subjectivity as that which is subtracted from the self-sustained processes of subjectivation and desubjectivation. In this regard, the extreme conditions suffered in the *Lager*, even

109

though they portray the misery of humanity and the plunder of the human attributes of man, reveal nevertheless a structural condition: the non-human is not the flip side of the human but, on the contrary, that which inhabits it. The same thing occurs with the processes of desubjectivation-subjectivation in relation to being the subject of the subject and the same can be emphasised in relation to the *not-said*: it does not constitute the other of language but instead, from the ends of the symbolic, harasses the production of signifiers.

Thus traumatism, even if it operates as exterior excitation, raises a decision in the subject that implies an internal resource in order to confront it. It is even clearer when the threat operates from within, from the libido itself. This discussion around the inner or outer origin of trauma was at the basis of all writings about war neurosis during the First World War.

In 1918, the Fifth International Congress of Psychoanalysis took place in Budapest, with many contributions dedicated to the theme of war neuroses, with papers by Freud, Simmel, Jones, Abraham, Ferenczi, and others. The Congress attracted not only the burgeoning psycho-analytical community but also officials from different governments (mainly Austrian, German, and Hungarian) who were interested in implementing specialised centres to treat that particular type of neurosis. It took place in the luxurious Hotel Gellért, and the event was of such magnitude, gathering so many spheres of Hungarian society, that Freud suggested to Abraham in a letter dated 27 August that Budapest had become the "centre of the psychoanalytical movement" (quoted by Stanton, 1997, p. 27). There was great social activity, and the years 1918 and 1919 were favourable to Ferenczi's leftist ideals, with Béla Kun as leader of the communist party, a situation which did not last more than a year when Admiral Miklós Horthy took power by force (1919 was also the year Ferenczi married Gizella Pálos). Ferenczi had been working with war trauma victims since 1915, first at the frontier in Pápa and from 1916 onwards as director of a neurological clinic in Budapest. He became passionately interested in war neuroses, which led him to an intense literary output, the most decisive of which, regarding war trauma (we must make clear that the theme of trauma, although not necessarily related to war, is present in practically all his work), appeared in two articles: "Two types of war neuroses (hysteria)" (1916) and "Psychoanalysis of war neuroses" (1918), the latter read at the 1918 Congress in Budapest.

It is striking, and at the same time disconcerting, to note how little the papers of that Congress contributed to the treatment of war neurotics. Perhaps only Simmel's paper offers clear references in this regard, but his therapeutics hardly inserts itself into the logic of the psychoanalytical movement, encouraging a series of pseudo-conversations on the patient's path from his profound hypnosis to his awakening. Although none of the other speakers defended a therapeutic method like Simmel's, the majority did come together in relating the appearance of symptoms of the neurotics with a narcissistic wound.

In "Two types of war neuroses (hysteria)" (1916), an article prepared for a lecture he gave at the María Valeria Military Hospital, Ferenczi attempted to distinguish the cases of war neurosis that are closer to the "conversion hysterias" than the so-called "anxiety hysterias". He considered that certain cases of neurosis could be understood within Breuer's and Freud's model of conversion hysterias: a trauma is produced by a sudden affect that exceeds the capacity of the psyche to cope with it. The psychic innervations adopted by the body at the time of the traumatic event prevail pathologically. Consequently, the sudden affect produced by the trauma remains in force and continues to produce effects at the unconscious level. Ferenczi classified the "mono-symptomatic" war neuroses as conversion hysterias. In the latter, the patient suffers a shock, followed by paralysis that eventually yields to reveal the innervation symptoms of certain specific organs. These would correspond to the "conversion hysterias".

There is, nonetheless, another type of clinical picture. Ferenczi considered that there are certain cases in which the attempt to perform certain acts triggers affects of anxiety, which he termed anxiety hysteria. For him, these patients suffer a series of psychic traumas that lead them to break their self-trust. The affects of these traumas are rejected to the unconscious, reducing the capacity for action. When realising that a series of events can bring the traumatic situation back, their only response to the environment is one of anxiety. The patient then becomes a kind of expert in avoiding acts associated with that repetition of the traumatic situation. Ferenczi referred to the advanced stage of this phenomenon as *astasia abasia*. These patients can exhibit hyperesthesia of the senses and present constant sleep disorders and impairment of their libidinal and sexual life. Thus for Ferenczi (1916): "we have the right to regard every case belonging to this group of war neuroses as an *anxiety hysteria*, and to consider the motor disturbance as an expression of phobia that serves the purpose of preventing an outbreak of anxiety" (p. 135, italics in original). Ferenczi believed that trauma produced a neurotic regression expressed in retreat at the onto- and phylogenetic levels, reading the difficulties of walking as a regression to a period prior to having gained the ability to walk and, at another level, prior to the ability to stand.

In addition, we observe that Ferenczi availed himself of Freud's contributions to the theory of trauma, considering that when a person manages to prepare himself for shock, mobilising affects while awaiting the event, he can counteract the observable effects in traumatic neurosis. He also sustained Freud's observation that a wound in the body can play the same role as the libidinal investment of the psychic system (it is amazing to see the extent to which this work regarding war neurosis predicted, and at the same time contained, the root of what will become Freud's (1920g) epistemological turn). For Ferenczi, in anxiety hysterias there is no possibility of locating the effects of trauma, the victim exposing himself to a traumatic situation unprepared and without bodily injuries. Even if these patients are able to realise the danger ahead, they are not capable of producing sufficient intensity to counteract the shock. As a result, the psychic system, left in a state of imbalance, requires an adjustment which is

> only possible when consciousness too becomes aware of the source of pain; this is then achieved by a certain "traumatophilic" attitude—the hyperaesthesia of the senses which in small doses gradually allows just so much anxious expectation and shock to reach consciousness as was spared to it at the time of the shock. In the constantly repeated little traumata, in each expectation of contact, in each little sudden noise or light, we should—following Freud's assumption—see a tendency towards recovery, a tendency to the equalizing of a disturbance in the distribution of tension throughout the organism. (1916, p. 139)

The person who introduces the term "traumatophilia" is Abraham (1907), using it to refer to a subjective predisposition that precedes all sexual trauma of childhood. Fenichel, on the other hand, also refers to traumatophiliacs[1] and reads in them the ineffectiveness of repetition as a mechanism of abreaction of trauma: "[…] the Ego desires repetition to solve a painful tension but repetition is in itself painful […]. The patient has entered a vicious circle. He will never be able to control the trauma by means of his repetitions, since each attempt brings in a new traumatic experience" (quoted by Laplanche & Pontalis, 1996, p. 254). Thus, the spectrum of the symptomatology of these patients is the ornament of its curative process, enveloped, nonetheless, in a diabolical circle (*Teufelskreis*). The same can be read in traumatic dreams according to Freud in *Beyond the Pleasure Principle* (1920g). In this way, that which the patient complains of—fear, the effect on his organs regardless of his will—is the phenomenon that he maintains through consciousness to facilitate his cure. There is an attempt, as Abraham also states when he refers to the behaviour of persons sexually abused during childhood, to display in a conscious scenario that which corresponds to primitive experiences. The eternal return of the traumatic, in its circularity, seeks nothing less than to turn that repetition of the same into a repetition of the difference, in the manner of a spiral. It is within this logic that Ferenczi reads those supposedly positive effects in which the neurologists of his time delighted: the electric discharge of electroconvulsive therapy would serve as nourishment in that search for pain as a way to deal with the suffering endured, its *traumatophilia*, but placed at the service not of curing the trauma but of a power system that demanded that its men return to the battlefield.

At the Fifth International Congress of Psychoanalysis, Ferenczi presented his paper "Psychoanalysis of war neuroses" (1918). His presentation started with an observation regarding the Russian revolution and revolutionaries' surprise at the fact that their actions did not have the rapid results intended through plans based on Marxist historical materialism. On the contrary, others seized power and, as happens time and again with countercultural movements, they ended up repeating the very things against which they had revolted. As Ferenczi mentions, the leaders of the revolution, seduced by the economic machinery and the systems of power, forgot "one small matter": nothing less than the psychic element of the revolution. Faced with the evidence of their omission, the Russians resorted to German works that reference knowledge of the psychic world, in order to put themselves on guard against that which had run through their fingers.

In his paper, Ferenczi took the opportunity to launch a harsh attack on an eminent contemporary neurologist who, like psychoanalysts, was involved in traumatic neurosis. Unlike them, however, Hermann Oppenheim, the first person to define traumatic neurosis in 1889,

114 CONFUSION OF TONGUES

considered that what produced neuroses were "physical alterations in the nervous centres, (or in the peripheral nerves which secondarily affect those of the centre)" (Ferenczi, 1918 p. 6). Ferenczi did not tolerate these simplistic notions, so popular among the doctors of his time. He stated that Gaupp considered "such specious physical and physiological speculations as brain mythology and molecular mythology. But in our opinion he does mythology an injustice" (p. 7). Later he named the way in which Oppenheim produced his theories, which resulted in an increasingly longer list of typical syndromes produced during the war, such as "Akinesia amnestica, Myotonoklonia trepidans", without these pathologies contributing much, according to Ferenczi, to the treatment or mental health in general, nor being in themselves particularly seductive. After that, he invoked, in a footnote, a supposed critic—who might be Ferenczi himself—who suggested using Oppenheim's words, difficult to pronounce, "in the examination of paralytic disturbances of speech, so that they might at least be of some good" (p. 7). Ferenczi availed himself, therefore, of his own dark humour as a rhetorical device to create awareness with respect to his discoveries in the battlefield. This does not mean that he was a sceptic of science. Just like his Viennese teacher, he envisioned future empirical corroboration of his psychoanalytical suppositions, especially those that related to quantum or psychic energy.

In his Budapest paper, Ferenczi made a theoretical journey in order to sustain the role of the psychogenic factor in traumatic neuroses, from Strümpell's objectionable mechanical-organic notions to the soothing writings of Mörchen, Bonhöffer, and others who pointed out that war prisoners did not present traumatic neuroses, statements that, even though they gave some weight to theses in favour of the psychic role in traumatic experiences, were, however, contested by the clinical experience of the years that followed. The discussion that Ferenczi introduced then centred on the predisposition of war neurosis. He affirmed that Gaupp as well as Laudenheimer, among others, considered that the traumatised subject was, from the start, neurotic, and that the traumatic event was nothing less than the trigger of a structural condition. Authors like Nonne, however, attached more weight to the traumatic event than to individual predisposition. Ferenczi, for his part, resorted to Freud's concept of "etiological equation"[2] according to which traumatism and structural predisposition play an important role and inversely complement each other in the emergence of war neuroses.

But psychoanalysis has not contented itself with a theoretical allusion of this relationship, but endeavors instead—with success—to decompose the complex notion of the "disposition" into simpler elements and establish those constitutional factors that influence the choice[3] of neurosis (the special tendency to fall sick with this or that neurosis). (Ferenczi, 1918, p. 13)

There appear, nonetheless, some nuances, since in certain cases, Ferenczi himself considered that trauma can come about despite the fact that there is no constitutive factor at play. In "On the psychical consequences of 'castration' in infancy" (1917), Ferenczi considered castration as something structural, which only in certain cases can become a concrete fact in reality, as in badly performed circumcisions or other genital surgery.

The First World War led to a practically unlimited quantity of literature related to traumatic neuroses. Ferenczi quoted Stern's work on the treatment of war neurosis in military hospitals from the perspective of the psychoanalytic model. He also referred to Mohr's work, which suggested treating war neurosis using the cathartic method developed by Breuer and Freud. In this way he attempted to revive the traumatic event so that the patient could repeat the emotion suffered at the moment of the trauma, thus achieving his abreaction. But, according to Ferenczi, the only person who had methodically applied what he termed *psycho-catharsis* was Simmel, who also presented his paper at the Budapest Congress. According to Stanton (1997), "War neurosis had been previously studied as 'battle hysteria'. In 1918, Babinski and Froment had even suggested that the phenomenon be incorporated within the general notion of 'suggestion'. They also believed that it was contagious" (p. 194).

Ferenczi analysed the role of inconsistency in the intensification of the symptoms. For Goldscheider, Aschaffenburg, and others, Ferenczi explained, falling unconscious during the traumatic event protected the subject from neuroses. Other authors, such as L. Mann, defended the opposite view and considered losing consciousness from Breuer's model of hypnoid states: loss of consciousness would lead to the impossibility of dealing with any component of affective overload. Nonne contradicted these arguments, however, since he believed that the unconscious continued to be vigilant despite the fact that consciousness was in repose. Nevertheless, Ferenczi discarded Nonne's theories on the basis that they resorted to a fairly limited notion of sexuality and eroticism, which associated sexuality to genitality, thus evading a more comprehensive idea of eroticism, according to what was presented in Freudian work. For Ferenczi (1918), Orlovsky is the one who

> expresses himself the most rationally on this vexed question; he points out the possibility that the swooning itself can be a psychogenic symptom, a flight into unconsciousness, which would spare the person concerned the conscious experiencing of the painful situation and sensations. The possibility of the psychogenic formation of symptoms during a faint is quite comprehensible to those of us who are psycho-analysts. This problem could be started only by authors who take up a standpoint, obsolete to psycho-analysis, that equates mental with conscious. (p. 17)

In his Budapest presentation, Ferenczi analysed in depth the mechanisms at play in war neuroses, which he had commenced working on in his article "Two types of war neurosis (hysteria)" (1916). He considered that in the cases of war neurosis not only the genital libido intervenes but something previous related to narcissism, giving an important twist to his theory by placing traumatic neurosis in the same spectrum as *dementia praecox* and paranoia. According to Ferenczi, a regression to a developmental stage, which he termed "love towards self", would occur, in which the patient's libido is stored in the ego, producing the demand that the other indulge, caress, and take care of him as if he were a small child. Such *estasis* of the libido in the ego leads to a decrease of objectal libido and, therefore, to a reduction of erotic investment in the objects of the world. However, for Ferenczi, no one was safe from contracting a war neurosis or from the functionality of such mechanisms, since each subject has narcissistic nuclei that, depending on the intensity of fixation to them, will require greater or lesser traumatic *quantum* to trigger a pathological picture.

If the presentation of symptoms was closer to phobia, that is, if the organic innervations aimed at *avoidance of repetition* of the traumatic event, Ferenczi considered them as anxiety hysterias. However, if the symptoms aimed at *repeating* the situation at the moment of the traumatic event, he considered them conversion hysterias. This difference between "anxiety hysterias" and "conversion hysterias", however, has remained in silence in psychoanalytic theory. More than because of its nosologic or diagnostic significance, it is of interest because of the novelty it introduces regarding thoughts about anxiety. Ferenczi's approach allows us to make a distinction with what will later be developed by psychoanalytic theory regarding anxiety since, to a certain extent, phobia as well as conversion offer objects for a "making with" such anxiety. In other words, there is a representation for anxiety to lodge in, even if the meaning of that representation escapes consciousness. But there is a dimension of anxiety that is anxiety as such, which does not fix itself to any object and, therefore, is unnameable and unrepresentable. This is the anxiety that will be developed later on in psychoanalytic theory, opposing it to fear, which, as "improper anxiety", *does* provide an object to the production of anxiety. (Even then, we should not lose sight of the fact that anxiety is, in itself, already an answer.) The latter, for its part, following a journey that makes its clearest appearance in the works of Heidegger and Lacan, is what exposes man to his essential decision: to continue or not to continue to exist (and, for Lacan, an anxiety that does have an object, of unique characteristics, which he names *object a*). These Ferenczian developments around the "anxiety hysterias" and the "conversion hysterias" are useful for this study insofar as they reflect the distinctive logic that Ferenczi employed as he considered in greater depth the causes of war neuroses.

In response to the suggestion that what traumatised neurotics searched for was a side benefit, such as a pension or a compensation on the part of the state or the armed forces, Ferenczi stated that these requests were only secondary to a stronger interest: the wish to remain safe from the situation that they felt had made them ill. Anxiety dreams were the subject's attempts to spontaneously cure himself from the illness acquired on the frontline.

There are two other articles by Ferenczi on the topic of war neurosis: "On the psychical consequences of 'castration' in infancy" (1917), which we have already mentioned regarding the Freudian "etiological equation", and "An attempted explanation of some hysterical stigmata" (1919), where he compares the causality of certain pathological phenomena, distinguishing them from the phenomena of religious stigmata in hysteria and a case of hemianaesthesia: the latter entirely due to the effect of the traumatic event and the former as a disposition of the body, as the result of the religious inclinations of the person who suffers them.

The function of anxiety in war neuroses

"In the moment of trauma, the world of objects disappears partially or completely: everything becomes objectless sensation."

Ferenczi, "Notes and fragments" (1932c, p. 261)

As previously mentioned, the First World War produced a vast number of war neurotics. As a result, there also appeared innumerable speakers who debated the origins of this pathology. Clarity regarding etiology meant pretending to be capable of distinguishing ill patients from simulators, similarly to what had been attempted some years back with regard to hysterical patients.

In this debate, Freud was summoned as an expert on the matter, in order to issue a recommendation with regard to accusations being made against the psychiatrist Julius Wagner-Jauregg, on the part of Walter Kauders, for having used his profession to treat war neurotics who were simulators and having used electroconvulsive therapy in an irresponsible manner. Wagner-Jauregg and a few like-minded neurologists had made of neurosis an organic condition, relegating the function of the psyche, in a similar manner to Oppenheim's theories. Freud, although he did not directly attack Wagner-Jauregg, was severe in his opposition to the use of electroconvulsive therapy, considering that it was not employed in the best interests of the patient but rather in favour of those in power, whether the state or the armed forces. When the question was posed whether these patients were war neurotics or simulators, Freud's answer foregrounded the issue of the profound sleep of hypnosis in which all neurotics find themselves since, to a certain extent, neurosis is always a simulation that operates regardless of the (conscious) intentions of the patient. Neurosis, in this sense, is an unconscious simulation and, in Ferenczian terms, the treatment and the work of the therapist are on the side of de-hypnotising. The debate with respect to the reality or the simulation of war symptomatology is not settled, and is still valid today. Professionals who work with traumatised members of the armed forces and the police are undoubtedly pressured by those institutions to determine to what extent these patients are genuinely seeking a pension or a way out of the institution. Unfortunately, mental health practitioners and psychoanalysts have not, throughout the history of the movement, been exempt from putting themselves at the disposal of dark systems of power; some macabre examples are the war psychotherapy supporting National Socialism led by Matthias Heinrich Göring, and the selection by Wolf Kemper, on the instructions of the *Wehrmacht*, of people with "abnormal psychisms" to lead multitudes into the gas chambers.

The papers presented at the Budapest Congress of 1918 were published a year later in a small volume of the *Internationaler Psychoanalytischer Verlag*, which had been recently founded. For its introduction, Freud draws up a short work entitled "Introduction to *Psycho-analysis and the War Neuroses*" (1919d). In it, he refers to the difference between war neuroses and transference neuroses. This discussion arises in relation to the place that threat occupies as a producer of anxiety: in the former, threat appears as an exterior danger, while in the latter the libido operates as inner danger. Freud states that

> [i]n traumatic and war neuroses the human ego is defending itself from a danger which threatens it from without or which is embodied in a shape assumed by the ego itself. In the transference neuroses of peace, the enemy from which the ego is defending itself is actually the libido, whose demands seem to it to be menacing. In both cases the ego is afraid of being damaged—in the latter case by the libido and in the former by external violence. It might, indeed, be said that in the case of the war neuroses, in contrast to the pure traumatic neuroses and in approximation to the transference neuroses, what is feared is nevertheless an internal enemy. The theoretical difficulties standing in the way of a unifying hypothesis of this kind do not seem insuperable: after all, we have a perfect right to describe repression, which lies at the basis of every neurosis, as a reaction to a trauma—as an elementary traumatic neurosis. (p. 210)

In this way, Freud appeals to a more comprehensive reading of trauma: repression is the evidence of trauma, its motor and its origin. Later traumas, whether caused by exterior or inner excitation (all of them being, nevertheless, somehow interior) would be the re-edition of that original trauma.

During the Congress, Freud studied the function of the traumatic dream and the role of repetition in the elaboration of trauma, referring at the same time to Ferenczi and Simmel's work in this regard. On this subject, both Ferenczi and Freud returned to Freud and Breuer's work regarding the memories suffered by the hysterical subject, according to the way in which the material of the neurotic had been interpreted in those years at the turn of the century.

In *Beyond the Pleasure Principle* (1920g), Freud mentions that war neuroses could be "traumatic neuroses which have been facilitated by a conflict in the ego" (p. 33). He states that mechanical commotion must be understood as a source of sexual arousal and, therefore, a wound (fever and aches) serves to redistribute the libido and ease the discharge of a *quantum* of that excitation. Traumatic action is produced by the lack of the subject's preparation (*angst* in opposition to *schreck*) when confronted by the traumatic event. This same mechanism operates for Freud in the way that certain organic illnesses cancel out the symptomatology of pathologies such as melancholy or *dementia praecox*.

When Freud works on the topic of the interior or exterior origin of trauma, he refers to what he calls *Reizschutz* or "the barrier against stimuli" (p. 29). This barrier offers the organism a protection against excitations from the exterior world. In economic terms, trauma is understood as the production of an excitation of such magnitude that it exceeds the subject's capacity to confront it by means of psychic mechanisms. Freud will give this a turn, however, in *Inhibitions, Symptoms and Anxiety* (1926d), when he refers to the way in which the ego, in a state of defencelessness, sets off an anxiety signal to defend itself from the automatic anxiety that attacks it, both from inside and from outside the psychic apparatus. It is also observed that unpleasant excitations from within the psychic apparatus are treated as exterior threats. Projection allows that which threatens to destablise the psychic apparatus from within, to be made into an external stimulus against which the "barrier against stimuli" is offered as protection. Trauma, being an excitation that exceeds the counteractable threshold due to this barrier, produces a flood of such magnitude that the psychic apparatus then tries to re-establish the previous homeostatic situation, an operation that works to the detriment of the functioning of other psychic systems. Thus, in the display, itself, of the symptomatology, it is possible to read, in turn, the operation of the defence.

The way in which Freud builds his theory of trauma after the epistemological turn of 1920 allows us to conclude that more than the fear or the panic triggered by the event, it is the lack of previous anxiety that sets the conditions for the possibility of trauma: the liberation of anxiety permits mobilising the systems of psychic apparatus in order to face the excitations that operate from without. That is also the objective of the traumatic dream: it tries to dominate the situation in a retroactive manner. The traumatic dream—which is not the same as the nightmare—offers the elements to prioritise the event, with sufficient anxiety to counter it. It is evident that here the pleasure principle no longer applies: there is an insistence on offering a return of the repressed material, nothing less than the compulsion to repetition.

Freud refers to how war neurosis is related to an experience of strong emotional content that, in general, spells danger for the subject who suffers it. His later evolution will consider whether trauma triggers the evolution of the symptomatology on the basis of a pre-existent neurotic structure or if the main determinant is not the structure but rather the traumatic situation itself. In the latter case, the symptoms would be essentially linked to the traumatic event, which returns time and time again in the traumatic dream as an attempt to link and discharge the overload produced by the trauma. In *Beyond the Pleasure Principle* (1920g) Freud explains that, even though traumatic neurosis is similar to hysteria, due to the quantity and diversity of motor symptoms, it manages to surpass it by presenting more marked signs and revealing greater subjective suffering (which remind him of symptoms such as hypochondria and melancholy). In addition, unlike hysteria, traumatic neurosis presents a greater impairment of the psychic functions and a more marked reduction of activity.

Even if Freud had not yet witnessed that which he foresaw in his later writings (*Group Psychology and Analysis of the Ego* (1921c), *Civilization and its Discontents* (1930a), "Why War?" (1933b), among others), namely, the magnitude of the Second World War and the passion for the abolition of the Third Reich, he did offer clinical and theoretical elements with which war survivors—and all those who demanded an explanation or wanted to understand what had occurred—could formulate some ideas around that which was unthinkable and unspeakable about the war. Of the survivors of concentration camps, in particular of Auschwitz, a group of thinkers appeared—Bettelheim and Primo Levi being just two of its exponents—who tried to symbolically order something of what was unexperienceable of the war. The Jewish holocaust was followed by work—literary, theoretical, philosophical, artistic, and filmic—that, despite its richness, has revealed up to what point trauma can be reduced to a narrative; precisely because such work introduces an excluded—impossible—dimension of the symbolic, it triggers an incessant, repetitive, and symbolic production that, even if it never succeeds in tackling its object, serves at least, at an imaginary level, to position it by drawing a kind of circle around it, besieging it (we find ourselves with a cultural and social mechanism that Freud had already placed intra-psychically in traumatic dreams). Within that logic, there were those who considered from the start that, because of its brutality, there was no possible word for the *Lager*, and that silence constituted the essence itself of reflection. Others, instead, despite starting off in that tradition, advocated the opposite: they considered that silencing the Nazi horror and the Jewish suffering was to comply with the mandate of the Third Reich and to worship what occurred in silence. Of the contemporary philosophers who have dealt with the topic of concentration camps and their implications, Giorgio Agamben undoubtedly stands out and, particularly, his book *Remnants of Auschwitz* (1999).

The untestifiable and the evidence of the subject

Agamben (1999) begins his work on Auschwitz by raising some sound criticism regarding how justice was handled with respect to the Nazis. He mentions that, despite the fact that the Nuremberg trials were insufficient, since they only sentenced a very small percentage of high officials of the Third Reich, they nevertheless gave the mistaken idea that justice had been done, that the barbarity of the extermination camps had been sufficiently dealt with. "With the exception of occasional moments of lucidity, it has taken almost half a century to understand that law did not exhaust the problem, but rather that the very problem was so enormous as to call into question law itself, dragging it to its own ruin" (Agamben, 1999, p. 20). Thus, a premise was established that contemporary mechanisms for resolving problems, put in place by countries in conflict (Latin American, among others), corroborate time and again: the search for the dissolution of conflicts has to choose either peace or justice, but not both; rather than going hand in hand, these two spheres repel each other in a reverse logic.

Agamben recovers, in depth, Primo Levi's work in order to think about a series of figures and events that took place in the concentration camps, Auschwitz in particular. He considers that Levi exposes man to a new ethical element that dynamites the very idea of responsibility, since in his work he refers to what he calls a grey zone, which makes certain instances, such as the victim and his executioner, good and evil, appear indistinguishable. "A gray, incessant alchemy in which good and evil and, along with them, all the metals of traditional ethics reach their point of fusion" (Agamben, 2000, p. 21). Agamben criticises the term "Holocaust" to describe the Jewish extermination, since this word comes from the Latin *holocaustum*, derived from the Greek adjective *holocaustos* (whose literal translation is "completely burned") and whose nominative form is *holokaustôma* (p. 28). The latter corresponds, according to biblical tradition, to a "total surrender to sacred and superior motives", undoubtedly an abhorrent way of designating hundreds of people entering a gas chamber. "Not only does the term imply an unacceptable equation between crematoria and altars; it also continues a semantic heredity that is from its inception anti-Semitic" (p. 31). The questioning of a theoretical system not only implies a revision of its concepts, but also of the hidden meaning of the terminology employed and of the particular logic upon which it is mounted.

It is well known that various intellectual circles considered that the barbaric events that took place in Auschwitz were of such magnitude that they could not be talked about. After Auschwitz, there would be no more poetry (Adorno). Thus, at the same time that something essentially human is buried in Auschwitz, what can possibly be said of it is also silenced, and, with it, the voice of its victims. As Agamben astutely points out, choosing not to speak of Auschwitz is giving status to *euphêmeîn*, the term from which the word "euphemism" derives, which colloquially aims at the substitution of one word by another for the sake of good manners. But etymologically, *euphêmeîn* means "to observe religious silence"; in other words, to enshrine for its glory. "We, however, 'are not ashamed of staring into the unsayable'—even at the risk of discovering that what evil knows of itself, we can also easily find in ourselves" (Agamben, 1999, p. 33). For this reason, Agamben cautions those who consider Auschwitz an unspeakable event. He considers it true that it was a unique event that will always expose—and must expose—its witnesses to a constant and active impossibility of speaking, but if these events are considered unspeakable in the sense that Auschwitz is an occurrence outside the universe of language, they would, despite their good intentions, be legitimising and putting into effect the very desire of the Nazis: that, after the war and despite its barbarity, the word of the survivor and the absence of testimony would silence forever the voice of the drowned.[4] To give testimony, on the other hand, is to give voice to the unpronounceable; it implies the possibility of displaying the tension, characteristic of all testimony, between the possibility and impossibility of saying.

The complete witness

Undoubtedly the most interesting and most profound thought in *Remnants of Auschwitz* is in Agamben's addressing the figure of the Muslim. *Muselmann* was the subject in the camp who had lost all of his human attributes. The camp prisoners saw in the Muslims the frontier between life and death and read in their faces their own possible destiny. At that frontier were those who could no longer react to any stimulus, who seemed to have lost all desire and all will, objects deprived of motor function, but who continued breathing with the slightest of movements of their organs. In the figure of the Muslim, the Jewish prisoners at the *Lager* were able to understand that humanity, and that which is human, are attributes that can be lost: what is human is a category that can be erased *from* the human. That a human belongs to humanity was something that the camp had managed to put into question.

> It is implicit in many testimonies that at Auschwitz everyone somehow set their human dignity aside. But perhaps nowhere is this expressed as clearly as in the passage in *The Drowned and the Saved* in which Levi evokes the strange desperation that overcame the prisoners at the moment of liberation: "Just as they felt they were again becoming men, that is, responsible ..." (Levi, 1989: 70, p. 59). The survivor is therefore familiar with the common necessity of degradation; he knows that humanity and responsibility are something that the deportee had to abandon when entering the camp. (Agamben, 1999, pp. 59–60)

The Muslim displays a grey zone, dead, where each man attends to the abolition of that which constitutes him as human and downplays the "being a man" of man. It reflects, like a perverted reverse eye, that the inhuman is not the outside of the human but its inseparable otherness, its most improper interior, its *extimity*. Agamben analyses the possible origins of the word "Muslim" to designate the drowned of the camps. The most probable seems to be the Arabic word *Muslim*, which refers to those who subject themselves without any preconditions to God's will. What is paradoxical about the term is that where the Islamic Muslim finds splendour in his commitment to Allah, the Muslim of Auschwitz presents a total lack of possible splendour or hope. As Kogon correctly points out (referred to by Agamben, 1999, p. 45), the Muslim's proximity to death was not an act of will but its loss.

Another origin, much less probable, of the word comes from *Muschelmann*, "shell-man," a man folded and closed upon himself (Agamben, 1999, p. 45). Des Pres' definition of Muslim is striking: "the empirical instance of death-in-life" (Des Pres, p. 99, quoted by Agamben, p. 92) (let us recall that Ferenczi had already described psychotics and later also his own traumatised patients as living dead). The fatality lies in the fact that Jews know that in Auschwitz they will not die as Jews but as Muslims.

In this regard, the Muslim appears as the untestimoniable of the camp. He escapes the word to such an extent that not even the SS officials knows how to name him, opting, when not to "cadaver" or "body", to *Figuren* (Agamben, p. 52).

> "The so-called *Muselmann*, as the camp language termed the prisoner who was giving up and was given up by his comrades, no longer had room in his consciousness for the contrasts good or bad, noble or base, intellectual or unintellectual. He was a staggering corpse, a bundle of physical functions in its last convulsions. As hard as it may be for us to do so, we must exclude him from our considerations." (Améry, quoted by Agamben, 1999, p. 41).

The Muslim was everyone's terror at the camp: a monstrous possibility (and the transformation into him imperceptible). It is surprising, in the series of narrations collected and quoted by Agamben, that the Muslim does not awaken either pity or mercy, but rather anger and contempt, not only amongst the SS officials but also among the prisoners of the *Lager*:

> "No one felt compassion for the Muslim, and no one felt sympathy for him either. The other inmates, who continually feared for their lives, did not even judge him worthy of being looked at. For the prisoners who collaborated, the Muslims were a source of anger and worry; for the SS, they were merely useless garbage. Every

group thought only about eliminating them, each in its own way."
(Ryn & Klodzinski, quoted by Agamben, 1999, p. 43)

The analysis of the Muslim undertaken by Agamben aims at seeing in him the threshold between man and no-man. Levi also aimed at this in his book *If This is a Man* (first published in Italian in 1958), to the point of asking himself if the death of the Muslim could be termed as such or if his death had occurred way before the cessation of his vital functions. Let us recall that Bettelheim himself conceived his institute for autistic children as an *anticamp* that would allow the alienated subjects to return to being men. He knew that trauma altered the order of things to such an extent that an opposite force was required that would push the trauma in the opposite direction. An extreme situation is, in a nutshell, that which executes the passage from being a man to becoming a no-man.

The Muslim, however, is not an other of man and neither is he the no-man of man: he does not exclude himself from man; they cohabit and they nourish each other. And possibly at this point it becomes impossible to turn one's gaze on the Muslim. Agamben relates how the liberation of Russians from Auschwitz was accompanied by film and photography cameras in the search for evidence for the future Nazi trials, images that reveal how it was not the pile of bodies that repelled the gaze of the cameramen but, instead, the presence of the Muslim.[5] Thus, "[a]ccording to the law that what man despises is also what he fears resembles him, the *Muselmann* is universally avoided because everyone in the camp recognizes himself in his disfigured face" (Agamben, p. 52). Everyone avoids looking at the Muslim, striving to make his presence disappear.

The Muslim, placing himself on the strip between life and death, reveals an even more horrific boundary: that of man and no-man. What is more, didn't malnutrition of the camp prisoners (well beyond an economy of food), which supposed a certain "regularity" of the bodies (similar in their thinness), make it easier for the SS officials to see them as generic beings, practically asexual, without age, thus avoiding that difference (singularity as apparition of one's fellow man) that would make it impossible to kill them?

Ferenczi's theory of trauma aims at an experience where the word has been lost, that is, trauma as such has been left outside the sphere of language. Lyotard is picked up by Agamben to think about how it is possible to speak of an experienced trauma if having experienced it inexorably exempts one from the possibility of giving testimony: human beings are always alienated from the possibility of bearing witness to their own history; to live that history is, from the start, to silence it. Lyotard refers to this rhetorically:

> "You are informed that human beings endowed with language were placed in such a situation that none of them is now able to tell about it. Most of them disappeared then, and the survivors rarely speak about it. When they do speak about it, their testimony bears only upon a minute part of this situation. How can you know that the situation itself existed? That it is not the fruit of your informant's imagination? Either the situation did not exist as such. Or else it did exist, in which case your informant's testimony is false, either because he or she should have disappeared, or else because he or she should remain silent. ... To have 'really seen with his own eyes' a gas chamber would be the condition which gives one the authority to say that it exists and to persuade the unbeliever. Yet it is still necessary to prove that the gas chamber was used to kill at the time it was seen. The only acceptable proof that it was used to kill is that one died from it. But if one is dead, one cannot testify that it is on account of the gas chamber." (Lyotard, quoted by Agamben, 1999, pp. 34–35)

As we have seen, entrance into language produces the symbolic universe, breaking up, at the same time, what could lie outside it. In this way, while it builds the symbolic, it also produces what is excluded from it, namely, its real. It is in this sense that the real can be also understood as production of language, even if it can never enter within it, at least not as word.

Bettelheim describes, as does Ferenczi, those beings whose vegetative life is the only evidence that therein lies something that is alive:

> "While his physical death came later, he became a living corpse from the time he assumed command of Auschwitz. That he never became a 'moslem' was because he continued to be well fed and well clothed. But he had to divest himself so entirely of self respect and self love, of feeling and personality, that for all practical purposes he was little more than a machine functioning only as his

superiors flicked the buttons of command." (Bettelheim, quoted by Agamben, 1999, p. 57)

And later:

> "Prisoners entered the moslem stage when emotion could no longer be evoked in them ... Despite their hunger, even the food stimulus reached their brain clearly enough to lead to action. ... Other prisoners often tried to be nice to them when they could, to give them food and so forth, but they could no longer respond to the emotional attitude that was behind someone's giving them food." (Bettelheim, quoted by Agamben, 1999, p. 57)

Another account quoted by Agamben reflects the nuances of that same effect:

> "They were so weak; they let themselves do anything. They were people with whom there was no common ground, no possibility of communication—this is where the contempt came from. I just couldn't imagine how they could give in like that. Recently I read a book on wither rabbits, who every five or six years throw themselves into the sea to die; it made me think of Treblinka." (Sereny, quoted by Agamben, pp. 78–79)

When analysing his patients' material in his *Clinical Diary* (1932b), Ferenczi stipulates what has been conceptualised as *splitting* (Gutiérrez-Peláez, 2006) and which has to do with a defence according to which the psyche, before eminent destruction, chooses self-destruction in order to save itself. Certain annihilation appears as a less anguishing terrain than waiting for uncertain death. As Lacan correctly rescues from Heidegger's writings, anxiety is that which drives the subject before the abyss of his essential choice: whether he continues or not to exist. Sure abolition, rather than a probable death, puts a stop to anxiety, de-territorialising it from the absence of co-ordinates; it promises a limited dimension against the limitlessness of anxiety.

Another topic that Agamben deals with extensively is the notion of testimony, since he finds in it the display of the paradox of language according to which one pretends to talk about that which one is not supposed to because it does not enter in the language. It is at this point that

Levi's phrase that designates the Muslim as a complete witness gains significance. The Muslim cannot speak, but he is the one who could say that which must be said: it is the Muslim who has lived; he is the one who has lived as a no-man. Here the lines between the Muslim and the *infans* become interwoven. Using Agamben's same logic with regard to the Muslim, we could say that Ferenczi's technical innovations are attempts by the psychoanalyst to allow the infant's testimony to appear. This does not mean unburying a trauma that occurred in the history of childhood but an awakening to the real of the trauma that makes of the *infans* the absent of the structure. But how does he who cannot speak bear witness? And how can someone else give evidence in his place if he has not experienced that which he is asked to testify about?

For Agamben, all writing and all words arise from testimony and, to a certain extent, the terrain of testimony is different from that of language and writing. The nature of the testimony is not displayed in the meaning of the words, since it is the lost of experience; testimony is, above all, the presence of the untestified.

> The language of testimony is a language that no longer signifies and that, in not signifying, advances into what is without language, to the point of taking on a different insignificance—that of the complete witness, that of he who by definition cannot bear witness [...] It is thus necessary that the impossibility of bearing witness, the "lacuna" that constitutes human language, collapses, giving way to a different impossibility of bearing witness—that which does not have language. [...] The trace of that to which no one has borne witness, which language believes itself to transcribe, is not the speech of language. The speech of language is born where language is no longer in the beginning, where language falls away from it simply to bear witness: "It was not light, but was sent to bear witness to the light." (Agamben, 1999, p. 39)

That no-language of language is evidence of the non-human that supports the human. Within every human being lies that absurd wound, like a Kafkaesque stamp that marks the vivid presence of the no-man.

If for modernity the subject was understood as fundamental, for contemporary thinkers like Agamben the subject is, instead, what remains as the result of a struggle between force fields. Thus, the question regarding the subject is not what constitutes his essence, his *entity*, but his *between*. The oppositional logic, so characteristic in the West, is sub-verted by a logic where opposites are not mutually exclusive but find their place in a struggle from which beings result. In particular, accord-ing to Agamben, the subject is the result of a struggle between a subjec-tivation and a desubjectivation. If language is understood as that from which subjectivities are constituted, it is necessary to position the mode of that language that deals with the subject, of the *between*—and here, once again, we express what we referred to previously as the "interme-diate language" (*Zwischensprache*), on the basis of what Benjamin stated regarding translation.[6] In this way, the subject appears in the move-ment subjectivation-desubjectivation, of the word to the no-word. The figure of the *in-fans*, he who does not speak yet, maintains a perma-nent tension with the speaking being. Similarly, Ferenczi's lost child-hood maintains a permanent tension with the speaker: the infant has become lost forever from the structure, but continues to produce effects on it, functioning as a hole. That tension speaks of trauma, namely, the trauma that implies the loss of the world in exchange for the word. The subject only exists as such in discourse, which has its (genealogical) origin in childhood.

Just as the child lives for his place in experience, the not-said awaits to appear in language. The not-said is not the negation of language but a kind of power of language itself, seeking the word. And even the power of the not-said is not one that fulfils itself with its transition to the act, since this is impossible (it is excluded from the structure, it dwells in the real), but is pure power that reveals the limits of thought. It is precisely towards the limit that experience is attuned: it detains itself before the first fruits of childhood. Consequently, power is the not-said that enables language.

The Muslim can be conceived from a psychological instance, as a trauma that took place in the history, early or late, of the living being, which leads him to such a state that it places him on the threshold of what is alive and what is dead, questioning the limit itself of what is human. But the Muslim can also be thought of as being in a structural place, as he who gives evidence of the articulation of man and no-man and how the no-man lives and is the power of what is human. Thus, as a lost instance of the structure, which not because it is lost—but precisely because of it—ceases to produce effects, it is a permanent strength of speaking beings. The *infans*, as evidence of the symbolic absence in all living beings (*zoé*), reveals that not speaking is also the possibility of all speaking beings, not as an instance which may appear by *anamnesis*, but rather as an experience of the limit, as the edge of the word, as an event. It is in this way that the Muslim approaches childhood: the Muslim does not speak because he denies himself to the word but because he withholds within him the not-said, what does not enter in discourse. The not-said is not that which excludes itself from the said. On the contrary, it is the no-word that speaks permanently in the word; it is its motor and producer, in the same manner that the Muslim is not the antithesis of the human.

As previously mentioned in relation to anxiety, extreme experience (that in the *Lager*, for example) exposes human beings to making a decision: to continue or to cease to exist. The life drive offers a way around that tragic death sentence. The living being is a being-towards-death; for Freud, what is lifeless is always there prior to life, awaiting as the aim of all life. Anxiety is what most draws the living being to the subjective experience, it is that which leads him to question being. For this reason, the death drive is a condition of the living being. Anxiety is that which, ultimately, decrees the imperative of responsibility. For the prisoners of Auschwitz, liberation made responsibility clear. Survivor's guilt relates to the feeling of occupying someone else's place. Evidence of this is Levi's poetry, illustrated in his poem "Dopo dí allora, ad ora incerta", where he writes: "I didn't usurp anyone's place. I didn't steal anyone's bread [...] It isn't my fault if I live and breathe, eat and drink and sleep and wear clothes" (Levi, quoted by Agamben, 1999, p. 90).

Thus, extreme experience, as a place of decision, implies responsibility before the other. But that decision does not necessarily mean excluding the other; on the contrary, it implies affirming what place the other occupies in me.

This dimension of guilt and shame is thoroughly studied by Agamben. What the liberation from Auschwitz by the Russians, on 27 January 27 1945, draws attention to is not the joy of men who are being liberated from enslavement but an amalgam of oppressed beings who slowly begin to feel the onset of shame. It is worth remembering what Ferenczi thought about guilt and shame in his studies on trauma. The victim, rather than feeling anger or hatred towards his oppressor, feels shame with regard to the facts. This is intensified, undoubtedly, if the adults who he loves or fears deny those events. In this way, it becomes easier to erase what has taken place, maintaining a favourable image of the adult—and with it a meaningful dimension of reality—rather than confronting the reality of the traumatic event. It is important never to lose sight of the fact that trauma does not reduce itself to the narration of the traumatic event: trauma will always be outside of the account and the narrative, regardless of the details the subject holds. The traumatic, by definition, excludes itself from remembrance. The traumatic is the other of representation, of the intelligible: it will always be outside of experience and will always be producing its effects.

Psychoanalytic theory, from Freud onwards, always ties the topic of trauma to that of remembrance. The traumatic experience starts making its havoc evident with the effects it has on memory. Is trauma something that can be remembered? What psychic status does it have? Is forgetfulness evidence against the existence of trauma or, on the contrary, is it the footprint itself of trauma? A characteristic condition of trauma is that it creates a certain unreality for the victim with respect to the trauma itself. "Even to us, what we had to tell would start to seem *unimaginable*" (Antelme, quoted by Agamben, 1999, p. 28, italics in original). Ferenczi deals extensively with the topic of trauma and remembrance. Explaining this phenomenon, he affirms that no register remains, not even in the unconscious, of the traumatic experience; the status of that traumatic material is not the same as what is repressed. Nevertheless, this does not prevent it from producing effects and formations of the unconscious. Trauma, in these terms, would refer to that which produces a hole that cannot be reduced to any representation whatsoever.

In this connection Levi's essential paradox gains meaning: *the Muslim is the complete witness*. He who cannot speak, who has lost speech having been stripped of his human insignia, he who reveals the non-man of man, is precisely the one who must raise his voice to speak about himself. Agamben expresses it as follows: *"The human being*, Levi's title [*Survival in Auschwitz*] implies, *is the one who can survive the human being"* (Agamben, 1999, p. 82, italics in original). The Muslim speaks from the frontier where what is human hides in the shadows. Such is the persistence of trauma that does not find a way of articulating what has occurred at the representative level. Once again, trauma appears as that which has been excluded from the psychic register, but from its absence it produces effects (at best, as symptom, but often as unconnected anxiety). Agamben's question is, then: How can we make that which has been left outside of the field of the word speak? How does the absent speak? And his shrewd answer is: It is precisely the absent that has been talking all this time. Testimony, ultimately, is always the testimony of the Muslim; what moves speech is nothing less. We need

Ermakov—a psychoanalyst who dedicated himself to war neuroses, treating soldiers during the war between Russia and Japan and who died in a Nazi concentration camp in 1942—to testify to his own experience. In him we have the complete witness to his own theories; Ermakov cannot testify about that which only he himself can testify about.

For Agamben (1999), "[f]rom this perspective, Auschwitz represents the historical point in which these processes collapse, the devastating experience in which the impossible is forced into the real" (p. 148). The real is understood here as reality, but precisely the fact that the impossible is introduced into reality implies a symbolic blurring in whose absence the real returns.

> Auschwitz is the existence of the impossible, the most radical negation of contingency; it is, therefore absolute necessity. The *Muselmann* produced by Auschwitz is the catastrophe of the subject that then follows, the subject's effacement as the place of contingency and its maintenance as existence of the impossible. Here Goebbel's definition of politics—"the art of making what seems impossible possible"—acquires its full weight. It defines a biopolitical experiment on the operators of Being, an experiment that transforms and disarticulates the subject to a limit point in which the link between subjectification and desubjectification seems to break apart. (Agamben, 1999, p. 148)

Thus we observe how Auschwitz exposes man against his real. Goebbels' machinery is a macabre use of technique to expose man before his real, which at this stage is the blacking out of all boundary between subjectivation and desubjectivation, since the real is not desubjectivation but the absence of pendular movement between one and the other. Schopenhauer also knew that life is a pendulum—for him, one between hatred and weariness. But when the pendulum ceases and the sore explodes, no man is left there, not even his flesh but his symbolic absence, his asignificance. Auschwitz, by forcing the sphere of decision to collapse, also brings down all possibility of producing sudden change: destroying the subject's temporality, it eliminates in turn all possibility of an event taking place.

Man's enjoyment is always inauthentic. Neither drive, nor language, nor the body belong to themselves. The Aristotelian definition of movement is fitting: things move because they are not where they should be. Thus, the maxim according to which desire is evidence of the banishment of enjoyment is always true. Man's being never inhabits his own house; human existence is the history of its own straying.

Event: what is excluded from the camp

The Japanese psychiatrist Kimura Bin (referred to by Agamben, 1999, pp. 125–127), director of the psychiatric hospital in Kyoto, avails himself of the various times of the *Dasein* to think about a series of pathologies. In order to do this, he picks up what he calls the *post festum*, "after the feast", and from there elaborates on the *ante festum*, the *intra festum*, and the *post festum*. Thus, he establishes that for melancholy, *post festum* applies, in the sense that what has already occurred is, for the melancholic, forever and remains eternal in immovable time. The *ante festum* takes place in schizophrenia, in the sense that the schizophrenic subject always arrives too early to his own feast; getting ahead of his own time of being, he is ruled by that permanent delay with himself. His life is always under the figure of anticipation because his ego is never there, under his wing, so to speak. For the *intra festum*, Bin provides two examples. First, he mentions the obsessive, who inhabits his own feast, but only at the expense of reiterating the obsessive act in time.

> The person obsessed with "taking full advantage" of time, or who governs his daily life with the imperative "time is money", only experiments "the improper of time", the exterior. He does not create it as event, he suffers it as an obsession. Asking about the "how" and the "when", the being-in-the-world loses *his* time. (López, 2004, p. 162)

In this way, what becomes useful for the obsessive is the strength of his obsession to dwell at his own feast, whose obsessive act is, paradoxically, a veil. The other example that he gives, stranger still, is that of the epileptic, where a kind of psychosomatic ego converges with an ego as entity of language. The overlap of the experience of these two egos, something like the grasping of the absolute present, leads the mind to its collapse, resulting in the epileptic attack. Here we can see that, somehow, Kimura Bin, despite resorting to Heidegger following the path traced by Binswanger, cannot escape the first Wittgenstein (1922), where there were *things* of the world that would acquire their equivalent in language through words and a *state of things* that would be referred to in discourse starting from the phrases that operate as articulators of those words. Even if that binarism—which excludes an absolute world that only touches man at a point that is language—pretends to be—and to a certain extent is—a mortal attack against metaphysics, it nonetheless offers the world up to empiricism in the sense that the *metaphysical* comprises all those words that do not have a referent in the world. Heidegger's attack against metaphysics, of quite different proportions, has to do with creating a path towards another way of thinking, not offering philosophy to instrumental reason but undermining reason in order to account for the unthinkable of reason itself, starting from that legendary oblivion where the question about the *what* has subsumed *being* to the essence of the entity.

What is interesting, and the reason why we mention Bin's use of the times of *Dasein*, is that he cleverly portrays the temporal lag, the gap between being and time in different entities of mental health. Obsessive neurosis is unaware of the gap that constitutes it and avails itself of the obsessive act in order to cope with its own castration. In this regard, Agamben (1999) affirms:

> In any case, according to Kimura Bin, man seems necessarily to dwell in a disjunction with respect to himself and his own *dies festus*. Almost as if living beings were constitutively divided on account of having become speaking beings, of having said "I", and as if time were nothing other than the form of this disjunction. And as if this disjunction could be mastered only in the epileptic excess or the moment of authentic decision, which represent something like the invisible architraves sustaining the ecstatico-horizontal edifice of time, keeping it from caving in on Being-There's spatial situation, its There. (pp. 127–128)

The time of the *Dasein* is not the time of the "cyclical repetition", that of Bin's obsessive, of free association; it is not that time where "the same temporal sequence is constantly repeated with the condition that this physical system is not subjected to change by any external influx" (Heidegger, quoted by López, 2004, p. 161), but that time "essentially inherent to experience as such, like its ways of giving itself, of the now, before and after, and the modalities determined by these, the simultaneously, the successively, etc. cannot be measured by the sun's position, nor with clocks, nor by means of anything physical, nor can it be measured in general" (López, p. 161); it is the time of the event, the *Ereignis*. For this reason, if temporality is introduced by language as a result of knowing oneself to be mortal, anticipating the uncertain but inevitable time of future finitude, the end of analysis occurs in that other time (depersonalisation and detemporalisation) where it is possible to proceed to the constitution of being. We understand, in this knowing ourselves mortal, the agonies of Borges' "immortal" (1949), who, unlike the animals, who are ignorant of their own finitude, is not eternal, but is condemned to an existence of knowing himself to be immortal, deprived of the delights of the *without-time* of animals. That metaphor of the end of analysis—"*poetic spark* which symbolizes a lack, but not with a signifier that we can interpret by *similitude* with that which constitutes it, but in the *maximum disparity*, that is, in the 'creation of a new signifier effect'" (López, 2004, p. 118, italics in original)—relates us not to the eternal return of Zarathustra's animals (Nietzsche, 1883–85), that tedious eternal return of the same, but to the eternal return of the different, according to what Deleuze rescues in his *Nietzsche and Philosophy* (1967).

Consequently, the event implies a kind of grasping of those different temporalities, of man's delay with respect to his own *dies festus*. Nevertheless, Auschwitz, having eliminated all temporality from the processes of subjectivation-desubjectivation, makes the advent of the event impossible. Therefore, the Goebbelsian mandate of *making possible the impossible* has been reformed into *making impossible the possible of the event*.

Returning to psychoanalytic writings, we note that traumatic neurosis implies exposing oneself to a situation for which one is not prepared. It is a scenario marked by repetition: that which cannot be remembered returns as repetition; that which the subject is ignorant of, returns time and again. Transference neurosis offers, in turn, a decisive component of repetition: with the analyst, the subject's previous transferences are repeated, revealing the resistential dimension of transference but, at the same time, it is thanks to this repetition that the functioning of repetition is located in the subject, opening the possibility of making transferential functioning conscious in order to free the subject from the diabolical circle. When we refer to the entrance of language, we do not find a dissimilar terrain: if the entrance into language is the unavoidable and constitutive trauma, we note that what permanently returns is the not-said, what is impossible to say, its significant silence. For this reason, before the mechanism of the death drive in repetition, it is not surprising that Freud distinguished the silence of that deadly drive.

What trauma demands, in its repetition, is to enter the symbolic universe. But the real of trauma will never enter language; the real does not allow itself in the symbolic, but at the same time plays an essential role in symbolic and imaginary organisation. Phenomenology, it has been suggested, consists in circling round the same tree time and again and at each turn finding a new branch. Repetition functions in a similar manner: the tree, in any case, is lost to experience; we are only left with its traces. Repetition leaves us with its attempt to link some signifiers and some representations. But, as such, trauma is precisely what escapes phenomenic experience, the symbolic, the representational, and in this sense it is consistent with Žižek's definition and development in relation to trauma and the real. Repetition is moved by a deception: somehow it thinks that it will carry out its function, and its insistence must be admired even if in the majority of cases its automatism becomes infinite, moving in an asymptotic manner without ever finding its parallel, namely, the real. We say that the automatism of repetition amazes us; its *automaton*, the insistence of its signs. But those signs cannot help entering somehow into the symbolic universe, whether by means of nosology, semiology, or some other nomination, universal or not. Lacan (1964, lecture 12 February), however, refers to that other way of repetition, the *tyché*, which would designate the real of the drive, the true motor of that insistence, its *impossible* in symbolic terms. We have already seen how the attempts to circumvent the Babelian confusion do not manage to surpass their own limits, since they are mounted on infinitisation. The examples worked by Umberto Eco (1993) reveal up to what point all attempts to provide universal solutions to the problem of the multiplicity of tongues, languages, and translations fail. Repetition, as *tyché*, speaks of what is lost of the structure, which, even though it cannot be symbolised, has nevertheless a fundamental function in the organisation of all symbolic and imaginary processes.

Traumatism speaks to us of the exterior event, but trauma is in itself the effect produced in the subject. Thus, we can see that even if Auschwitz produced a traumatism in the subjectivity not only of the prisoners of the *Lager* but also on the subjectivity of an epoch, it revealed, as probably other traumatisms have done throughout history, the existence, once again, of an *arch*-original trauma. This *arch* trauma—to which several psychoanalysts have wanted to attribute a symbolic place, whether as "birth trauma" or "weaning" or in other forms, including Ferenczi himself, to a certain extent, with his *Thalassa* (1924a)—only exists, however, as the figure of loss, and it is precisely because it is not there that we account for its existence. To a certain extent, the original *Thalassa* is pre-verbal and the confusion of tongues is the loss of that original sea, being, at the same time, the gain of the world that speaks, but a gain always mediated by the figure of the loss.

Even if Freud does not ignore the importance of particular experience, and the particularities of its effects on the subject, the clinical material of his sessions leads him to the discovery of a kind of fraternity of traumas. A trauma does not appear in isolation, but offers a network that interconnects it with other traumas. In this way, even the traumatism that occurred during the war, and which overwhelms the subject with total surprise, does not prevent it from being struck by elements specific to the subject (his *Empfänglichkeit*) for the production of trauma. The traumatic event does not exclude the dimension of desire; the subject is prone to trauma by the mere fact of speaking. Language, which produces the unconscious, mediates in the incorporation of experiences within knowledge. Thus, language offers, by its very existence, the conditions of trauma. The subject, being a speaker, dissolves all possible paths to his object of desire. He is only left with language as access to enjoyment, of which, nonetheless, the object of desire is lost. Language is also traumatism inasmuch as it produces an effraction of the subject, the opening of his fissure.

Fear, an improper anxiety

"The voluntary searching for, or even hastening of, the unpleasure has subjective advantages *vis-à-vis* what may be a prolonged expectation of unpleasure and death. Above all it is I alone who prescribe for myself the tempo of living and dying; the motive of anxiety about something unknown is shut out. Compared with the expectation of death coming from outside, suicide is relative pleasure."

Ferenczi, "Notes and fragments" (1932c, p. 244).

Fear is always fear of something, of an external object. Terror, on the other hand, implies recognising the feared of oneself in the other (finding the internal *daimon* in outsideness). Anxiety, however, implies confronting the vacuity of existence and, therefore, it forces a decision to continue or to cease to exist. Alemán (2003) addresses it as follows:

> in anxiety, for Heidegger—that is what Lacan will later recodify with anxiety and his theory of object *a*—we don't know what causes our anxiety, because in fact anxiety leads to oneself. Heidegger says that fear is an improper anxiety, and the latter that which leads to our essential choice because we cannot justify ourselves with that which makes us fearful, but with what we are ourselves. We are anxious because we are here, not because we are afraid of this or that. (p. 18)

When Ferenczi defines anxiety neurosis, he displays its mechanism according to phobic logic, but it is clear in his later writings that it is no longer with the objects of the world that the subject defends himself; what is at play is life itself as essential choice.

War neurosis, being an experience of anxiety and an extreme situation where the subject is defenceless, unable to put before himself a representation of, or a libidinal movement (investment) to, what presents itself to him, is confronted with that same decision. Thus, following the trail laid down by Ferenczi, we can formulate the hypothesis that war neurosis is associated with having taken the decision to not continue to exist and, despite it, having continued to live. Alemán (2003), appealing to the concept of Sartre's *decisionism*, expresses his view on the role of decision in anxiety as follows:

> Sartre has captured this because, for example, if one is in a concentration camp, or lives a totalitarian experience, it is true that one identifies one's enemies, identifies the terror and adopts the adequate physiognomy to hide oneself. But he also knows that when one has lived a situation of extreme panic, the choice of whether one will want to continue living or not is renewed more than ever; and that is the point of anxiety. Consequently, anxiety means extending the responsibility and not shielding oneself in bad faith. (p. 18)

Anxiety can be placed, therefore, in relation to decision-making. Ferenczi's question then becomes: How is it possible to go on living having rejected life as a possibility?

For this reason, it is useful to analyse a fragment of a session presented in his *Clinical Diary* (1932b). At the beginning of the diary entry for 30 July 1932 entitled "'Literal' repetition endlessly repeated—and no recollection", Ferenczi refers to his patient B who, after relating a dream, hits herself indignantly because there are things she cannot have access to via remembrance, but only through dreams. In response to this, Ferenczi says to her: "I know from other analyses that a part of our personality can 'die,' and if the remaining part does survive the trauma, it wakes up with a gap in its memory, actually with a gap in the personality, since it is not just the memory of the death struggle that has selectively disappeared or perhaps has been destroyed, but all the associations connected with it as well" (p. 179). The patient then asks him why, if she knows this, she cannot realise that she finally managed to survive and exist with that part of her personality. She asks herself why it is impossible for her to remember the past in a normal way, but can only return to it in that deformed or oneiric way. Ferenczi then replies: "I know from other cases that there can be frighteningly painful moments, in which one feels one's life so appallingly threatened, and yet oneself so weak or so exhausted by the struggle, that one gives up. In fact one gives oneself up" (p. 179). Then he refers to a case described to him by a friend of his, a Hindu hunter who witnessed the moment in which a falcon attacked a small bird. What was special about the tale was how the hunter observed that the small bird, seeing the falcon, started first to tremble and later dashed himself directly against the falcon's beak, who proceeded to swallow it. This image evokes a story by Hoffmann worked by Freud in "The 'uncanny'" (1919h) (the moment in which Nathaniel throws himself from the tower before the vision of the "beautiful eyes" of Coppelius), just like in Kafka's "The vulture" (1920), where a bird buries his beak in the mouth of the protagonist, only to die drowned in his blood: it is a double movement of liberation by death; both the vulture and the protagonist die, and in that death the protagonist is saved from the pain and torture to which the vulture subjected him: "Falling on my back I felt a kind of liberation; I felt that in my blood, which filled all the depths and inundated all the rivers, the vulture, inexorably, drowned." Ferenczi suggests that "the anticipation of certain death appears to be such torment that by comparison actual death is a relief" (1932b, p. 179). The same is evidenced in suicides that occur prior to a situation where death appears as a possibility (a duel, a war, or an execution). This depriving oneself of life is a relative relief when compared with the unbearable fact of an aggression that crushes and exceeds the totality of possibilities and resources one has available.

Ferenczi asks himself about the state in which the small bird in the previous example would find itself if it were rescued from the falcon at the instant before being swallowed. He asks himself about the state of his psyche and what it would do with the memory and his attempt to kill himself—"there would probably have remained only a memory; for what is remembering: the conservation of a memory trace for the purpose of future use" (1932b, p. 180): precisely as in the case of the small bird—which must evidently be read as similar to those of patients treated in Ferenczi' practice—who has renounced life and a future, has no more reasons for remembering anything, since he *has given up his soul*, has abandoned himself. In this way, if, thanks to his exterior forces or certain vital forces, he has managed to survive, despite having made the decision to die, the events that took place will, given the mental absence of the individual, only appear (if they do appear) as if they had occurred to someone else, since, in fact, at that moment the person *was not*. There will be cases in which "retreat from the patient's own self was so complete that even the memory of the entire incident was lost" (1932b, p. 105). Later, he affirms that the suffering is so unbearable "that a splitting of the personality results. On awakening the complete-ego cannot remember any of the events that occurred while it was split" (1932b, p. 170). The question then appears: how can we "render conscious what has never been conscious before? "(1932b, p. 181).

Following that path, Ferenczi involves the *Verleugnung* when he hypothesises two possible ways of dying: either resigning oneself to death or protesting against it to the very end, a protest that usually takes the form of the denial of reality, leading to mental disturbance. Total denial produces the *vanishing*, and partial negation the replacement of reality by the dream (again the dimension of sleep). It is observed, in Ferenczi's patient mentioned earlier, however, that there is an impossibility of setting aside that split part of her personality, affirming that the "split-off part seems to represent in the first instance a large, indeed perhaps the most significant, part of my soul, and even if you were to urge me to, which I hope you will not, I should never stop striving to make that portion of my personality, however painful, consciously my own" (1932b, p. 181), evidencing at this point that it is precisely anxiety that operates as co-ordinate, making it impossible for the patient to put her suffering aside. Even though the conscious memory does not appear, a certain present affectivity is manifested that highlights the presence of that split. For this reason, there is no representation whatsoever, but the presence of an affect is shown and this particularity led Ferenczi to ask himself whether what was at play there had to do with repression.

Ferenczi observes in his patients a permanent attempt to recover that lost part of their being: "this personality, shattered and made defenseless by suffering and poison, is attempting, over and over again but always unsuccessfully, to reassemble its various parts into a unit, that is, to understand the events taking place in and around her" (1932b, p. 158). Nevertheless, that attempt is in vain, with fragmentation again operating on each occasion. For this reason, Ferenczi emphasises the importance of an analysis that allows the patient to relive the trauma in order to experience it in the analytic relationship and in transference.

Ferenczi's patients move permanently between those polarities: unity and fragmentation, approach and withdrawal regarding anxiety, grasping, and letting go of themselves. Thus, at the moments of analytic regression "... [they] feel only an utterly unbearable quiet, which [they] fear more than anything else" (1932b, p. 198). It is the fear that appears before reliving the trauma, before the *experiencing* of that which cannot be remembered for having been left without any register whatsoever of the event. During certain moments of the session, Ferenczi's patient has some recollections of her crisis but, once they are incorporated, the memories of the aggressions she has evoked from childhood become unreal: she ignores how something of the trauma seems untouched by her narrative and her representation. His patient fantasises that, as long as a certain union of her split parts is impossible, it will likewise be impossible for the crises that she has experienced from time to time to turn into true memories; but, as we have seen, the *Urbild* is not reconstructed by the sum and assembling of the split-off parts.

When Nietzsche advocates the death of God, he aims at dismantling everything that could be termed *deontometatheology*. As an ethical stance, religion maintains the sophism that without God and without law men would annihilate themselves (let us remember the *God is dead, everything is permitted*, attributed to Dostoyevsky, and the Lacanian *If god is dead, nothing more is permitted*). Atheism, understood as the renunciation of that *Urbild*, allows us to found another type of ethics. For Sartre, "'True atheism [...] occurs when the concept of responsibility is finally extended; one is truly an atheist when he has shown that, in life, responsibility gains prominence'. This would be the major thesis of his manifest" (Alemán, 2003, p. 14). We have already seen how responsibility is precisely what comes up as reality for the liberated prisoner at the camp.

In this way, we find the ethical ground upon which to place what Alemán has elaborated regarding anti-philosophy: an ethics founded on the (structural) hole of ex-istence. Thus, extending the reach of responsibility before the question *Why not kill the other?*, it is possible to answer with a *Because I can*; not killing him precisely because killing him is inserted within my frame of possibility. It is a reverse logic to that of the perverse individual (religion, which supposes an Other who always knows what is best for us—until even its place is confused, affirming that religion itself is what is best for us—is inserted within that perverse logic). A very telling definition of perversion, precisely because of its apparent simplicity, is the one offered by the British psychoanalyst Adam Phillips (1994), when he affirms that perversion is: "knowing too exactly what one wants, the disavowal of contingency, omniscience as the cheating of time; the mother who, because she knows what's best for us, has nothing to offer" (p. 108). For Phillips, perversion has to do with knowing (or thinking we know) too well what the other needs. In this way, true atheism could be placed at the antipodes of this: where the perverse individual knows *quite well* what the other enjoys, the atheist would not put anything before the enjoyment of the other, since that would imply, in Levinasian terms, killing the other's *otherness* and making it sameness of my own objects, chosen from the basis of a metaphysical framework.

The concepts that have been presented throughout this journey, namely, war trauma on the one hand and language trauma on the other, acquire an intimate relationship with respect to the *Dasein*, inasmuch as the latter places man in relation to the uncertain future of his non-existence, uncertain as temporality, but not as certainty of the event: *Do men attend their own death?* Wanting to be alive when one dies is, undoubtedly, a romantic ideal. In a fragment of his autobiography (which was never published, but if it had been would have been called *Not Less Than Everything*), quoted by his wife Clare, Winnicott himself exclaims to an imaginary T. S. Eliot "Oh, God! May I be alive when I die" (Winnicott, C., 1989, p. 4). The entrance into language (the traumatic dimension of language; Gutiérrez-Peláez, 2015) is precisely what ensures that certain but indeterminate time of one's own death, the future finitude. Thus, *the awakening to the confusion of tongues* is what allows true atheism, outside of the avatars of metaphysics. Not for this reason does it cease being a semblant (even Nietzsche in his *Posthumous writings* (2006) appealed to the need for postulating a *subject* for thought, regardless of whether that subject had a fictional status; a logical necessity, but nevertheless a non-totalised or totalising subject), but it does allow the exposure of the opening, the wound, the fissure towards the real of trauma, to the real dimension of trauma. We say that it does not cease from being a semblant, but it is undoubtedly a very different one to that built by the subject with the narrative of the trauma.

Thus, arriving once again at the Ferenczian conceptualisation of the confusion of tongues, it would seem paradoxical that these two modes of trauma (language trauma and war trauma) should be assimilated, considering that one apparently leads to the acquisition of language and the other, on the contrary, manifests itself as loss of the word, as impossibility of saying, of naming. But this opposition only *appears* to be such, since the trauma of language is also loss of the word, loss of those signifiers that could name something outside of the delimitation of the symbolic. The entrance of language always implies the loss of a world and makes of enjoyment that which never meets with its object. For Alemán (2003), "enjoyment does not express a force nor a first energy prior to discourse, since for enjoyment to exist, the living being must be caught by language, although the latter might not be able to signify it later" (p. 28). The paradoxical relationship, therefore, takes place between enjoyment and language, rather than between war trauma and language trauma, since to be able to speak of a subject who enjoys, it is necessary that a subject be taken by language that, in turn, could never signify that enjoyment.

CHAPTER THIRTEEN

The return to Ferenczi

Es gibt kein Höheres Recht, als das der Wahrheit.
[There is no higher law than that of truth.]
Ferenczi, "On sexual transitionary", 1906

After taking the journey we proposed, it is now possible to understand the importance and relevance of Sándor Ferenczi for contemporary psychoanalysis. His writings contain original and acute elements, allowing us to create a systematic return for our times. Throughout the previous chapters we have traced, extracted from, and conceptualised the Ferenczian notion of the "confusion of tongues" in order to propose new consequences of the traumatic dimension of language. It has also been possible to take up the Ferenczian oeuvre, highlighting the present in his writing, overlooked in previous readings that have been made of it.

This re-reading exercise allows us to establish significant differences between Freud's and Ferenczi's traumatic theories. Traumatism appears as the contingent fact that produces psychic commotion; trauma, on the other hand, is the effect that that contingent event has on the subject. During the first stage of his traumatic theory, Freud saw in remembrance the main tool that could weaken the repressions that persisted there, giving consistency to the symptom. But soon afterwards he abandoned

traumatic theory, producing an in-depth knowledge and a clinical practice that went beyond a therapy of memory. On a third journey in his
work, as we have attempted to indicate, the logic of the drive remnant,
which he names the death drive, appears in his writings of 1920, which
inscribe another mode of satisfaction: the deadliest aspect of the drive.

In 1931 and 1932, Ferenczi, for his part, was producing something
different from Freud with regard to his first traumatic theory. We
observe how Ferenczi was read by various contemporary psychoanalysts, including Freud himself, as a return to the first Freudian theory
of trauma. We were able to extract from Ferenczi's work the traumatic
place that has its topology in the threshold between sense and drive.
In addition, it was described how in Ferenczi there is the production of
something new that distinguishes him from Freud. Ferenczi installs a
difference despite, according to how he was read at the time, seeming
to return to Freud's first traumatic theory.

In this way, it is possible to establish two types of trauma in Ferenczi:
a trauma in reality *vs.* a structural trauma. The structural notion of
trauma is the effect of the word on the body, which becomes desiring
and sexed. Both "childhood" in Ferenczi and the "other" in Levinas
can be placed in a mythical time prior to the dimension of desire and
all of history. The fact that the adult addresses the "infant" simply by
talking to him installs the confusion of tongues. Trauma is understood
in this way as an effect of the real. A theoretical journey allows us to see
that a true encounter with the real never takes place; they are always
failed encounters.

In accordance with the relevance of returning to Ferenczi, the notion
of childhood has been read as a structural place: it designates the childhood that is always lost, free from guilt and desire. In that regard, it
has been possible to observe how, in Ferenczi, the other appears as the
limit of language: the other as the banished from language, its outlaw.
An important element specified in this study, and which marks a substantial difference with Freud, is the way in which Ferenczi reads the
deadly element all subjects possess as an effect of the other's action.

The re-reading has allowed us to specify three dimensions of the
confusion of tongues: an imaginary dimension, established between
the innocent child and the passionate adult who subverts that state; a
symbolic dimension, related to the confusion of tongues as metaphor,
according to Rachman (1989, 1997a & 1997b); and a real dimension,
namely, the traumatic dimension of language as such. Ferenczi names

that relation of kinship between trauma and language as a confusion of tongues. With respect to the traumatising agent, we suggested that it does not appear in the imaginary narrative of the traumatic situation but in the real that the imaginary relationship veils. Trauma is always outside the narrative that can be constructed from it, even if it is, at the same time, the possibility of constructing the narrative itself. That aspect was also worked using Benjamin's "The storyteller" (1936), when he referred to the absence of narratives on the part of war veterans.

This notion of trauma has been articulated with the myth of the tower of Babel, since it has an impact on the issue of the "confusion of tongues". Having journeyed down the path of this myth and studied the profound link with the issue of translation, we were able to raise a paradox: Babel imposes the need for a translation between tongues and, at the same time, it is because of Babel, as confusion, that such a translation is impossible. The tower of Babel, always understood as the *ruin* of the tower, situates the topology of the not-said of language. Just like the men of Nimrod and the other inhabitants of Babel, we are also unable to say it All.

With respect to the not-said of language, and availing ourselves of Levinas' philosophical contributions, we were able to infer that if language only spoke of difference, nobody would be able to understand the other: it would be a pure monologue of disparate spirits. However, language speaks of the same, but does this imply that the other disappears? Or does that dissymmetry of communication prevail in what is not said of language (in the not-said that dwells as presence in language)? Is that not the wager psychoanalysis makes: that desire, as the unyielding of the subject to the trickeries of sense, is always there, active, thriving between the signifier folds?

The myth of Babel was thus reinterpreted. The most significant aspect of the Tower was not its height but the space lodged at the centre. The huge enterprise was the creation of an empty vessel. Its essence was not given by what was built but by the void that surrounded what was built.

One of the main contributions of this journey relates to the articulation of the notion of "awakening", following J.-A. Miller (1986), with regard to the issue of the traumatic dimension of language. It is possible to see in Ferenczi's oeuvre his insistence on producing an awakening, retaking a path that he understood as contrary to hypnosis. As Ferenczi's own words, quoted in the epigraph to this book, suggest, he trains in the ranks of those who awaken.

Awakening is understood as a movement contrary to hypnosis. In his writings, Ferenczi highlights the de-hypnotisng aspect of psychoanalysis. His clinical work, profusely documented in his later writings, aims at the encounter of something unknown, in the order of the real and therefore anti-natural. The analyst's desire is precisely to produce an awakening, according to what was thought about and built in relation to Ferenczian work.

Just as with "awakening", "sleeping" to the real is a fantasy, an equally impossible ideal. Ferenczi aims at producing an awakening to a real: if with the signifier one sleeps, a mechanism must be found to boost an awakening to that real.

The psychoanalytical movement, for its part, can be read as an oscillation between sleeping and awakening. For this reason, the question addressed at the beginning of this book is relevant: Can Ferenczi be considered within or outside the psychoanalytical movement? History certainly tried to exclude him but the logic of his method, which is nothing less than following the path of the unconscious, intimately links him with the movement. His clinical and theoretical work is the result of his loyalty to the analytical method and to the foundations of psychoanalysis. In this regard, evidence indicates that Ferenczi anticipates certain psychoanalytic conceptions that will find their place much later on. With respect to the traumatic dimension of language in particular, it is Lacan who rescues its darkest tints, inserting his powerful concept of the Real in his triad with the symbolic and the imaginary, as nodal to the understanding of the imminently traumatic aspect of speech.

The re-reading of "Confusion of tongues between adults and the child" (1932a), enables us to understand that "confusion of tongues" is the name acquired for the traumatic dimension that insists in the real of language. Since psychoanalysis is a practice that takes place in language, it is continually challenged by this traumatic dimension. What Ferenczi outlined is always displayed in a clinical dimension. His perceptions and intuitions are the result of what he finds and analyses throughout his work as a psychoanalyst.

The confusion of tongues is traumatic because it implies a loss for all speaking subjects, but it is immanent to the confusion of tongues that the subject speaks. The "traumatophilia" is structural in all subjects simply due to the fact of speaking. Trauma is that which injects the monad of authenticity to all experience. For this reason, experience does not exhaust itself in sense.

Following the line of psychoanalysis as a practice of speech and recognising the traumatic dimension as nodal to clinical practice itself, we have
worked and reconstructed the notion of interlanguage (*Zwischensprache*)
from Benjamin's writings; this notion was articulated as a product of the
analytical journey. Interlanguage, as a major language, belongs to desiring and speaking beings; it does not exclude the dimension of desire
from its functioning. We desire *because* we speak, even if it would seem
that we desire *despite* speech. This intermediate language differs from
creative language, from the language of domination and communication, according to the way they were defined in Benjamin's writings.
The latter always implies the symmetry of the speakers.

The Benjaminian interlanguage pretends to include, as incessant
movement, the *not-said* as something different from the *outside* of language. The *not-said* of language is there inscribed as the untouched
of translation. In language there is always a presence of the different
from itself, of the quintessentially dissymmetric. That not-said is positivity of—and for—language. Intermediate language recognises such
positivity.

Just as the passage of languages produces a remnant that is positivity
and not a defect or mistake of languages, the subject is equally that which
appears as subtraction of a subjectivation process, incessant as the passage of tongues, incessant inasmuch as the subject speaks. The journey
of this investigation allowed us to conclude, with Agamben (1999), that
the subject appears as remnant of the subjectivation and desubjectivation processes. Taking up his work on the notion of the "Muslim" in
the Nazi concentration camps during the Second World War, it was
possible to study in depth the relationship between language and that
which is human, articulating it with the effects produced by trauma on
those instances. The parallels between the traumatised of the *Lager* and
Ferenczian patients, allowed us to delve into the effects of the confusion
of tongues as the real of language.

Passing from the trauma of language to the trauma of war was a
movement that allowed the clinical work of war neurosis. Even though
the literature regarding war trauma is not abundant in contemporary
psychoanalytic productions, there is research that evidences its relevance in the field (Gutiérrez-Peláez, 2017b). We also saw that even
if the first generation of analysts did not have methods at hand that
significantly favoured the treatment of war neurotics, it did analyse in
depth the nature of anxiety and its most representative variants. Those

developments regarding anxiety maintain their relevance, since they speak of the underlying emotions of all neuroses, linking their outburst to narcissistic mechanisms. It is striking that certain issues of psycho-analysis seem to vanish from the scene with the years. But the fact is that a return to those first writings of the agents of the movement, inso-far as it has been carried out by a reading attentive to the subjectivity of our time, has allowed us to enrich the epistemological and technical foundations of contemporary psychoanalytical clinical work in relation to the work on trauma developed by Sándor Ferenczi.

What can be said then in relation to the "experience" of the trau-matic dimension of language insofar as there are subjects who speak? We find that, inevitably, there is a dimension of experience that implies a subject that can withstand it. To make "experience" implies not reduc-ing something of the *experienced* to objective matter. At the same time, experience always occurs within language. But language is not only what is said. What is not-said does not oppose itself to what is said, but each interacts in such a way as to allow the absent of language to make its appearance in the construction of language.

Throughout this investigation, we have dealt with *experience* from two convergent places: on the one hand, from Benjamin's concepts, who suggests that there is a dimension of *experiencing* that is not exhausted in sense and which is evasive to the register of the signifier; and, on the other, in the presuppositions which we referred to as *antiphilosophy*, according to what Jorge Alemán rescues from Lacan. Antiphilosophy was undoubtedly an essential path in the work undertaken, but in no way does it end with this investigation. On the contrary, it will probably be a field of great richness for future investigations, offering a novel kinship between psychoanalysis and philosophy and placing psycho-analysis at its highest point of innovation with respect to the clinical practice and thought from which it commenced.

Alemán discovers antiphilosophy in the convergence Freud-Lacan-Heidegger. With respect to this convergence, we observe that when Heidegger raises his criticism of technique, he denounces the way in which the latter does not admit the impossible. If the impossible were admitted, technique would postpone its realisation: it refers to the place of the impossible as contingent and promises a future where the impos-sible will finally become territory of the possible. Thus, everything that is presented as impossible exists in such a way that the future will vindicate its possibility. Inasmuch as science is technique, it pretends

THE RETURN TO FERENCZI   151

to take possession of the absent of experience. In this regard, science as technique is pure metaphysics: it supposes a universe of closed ends and meeting points where the possible and thinkable come together in a perfect circle. All theism and all identity are a closure of experience and of the world; atheism, on the contrary, aims at an ethical opening towards the impossible. Just as Alemán (2006), from the point of view of antiphilosophy, suggests that democracy can only exist as long as "there is always a place which is impossible to fill" (p. 172), we can also say that science can only exist as possibility inasmuch as the impossible is not the outside of its co-ordinates. Science is similar to totalitarian systems, since it closes all possibilities of the void and the impossible taking place.

The subject, for his part, never names himself completely in the register of signifiers. There is always a split in that dimension, the reason why the subject does not reduce himself to representation. The ideal of the technique is that the world can be reduced to signifiers, expelling the impossible from the register of its interests. For this reason, the path traced in this investigation, guided by the concept of the "confusion of tongues" as conceived by Ferenczi, points in a very different direction from that of technique. Far from wanting to weld the issue of the subject as speaker in a paradise without splits, it is hoped that the opening and the impossible may find their presence in the register of language and of clinical practice, even if this always occurs in a failed manner.

As Milner (1978) correctly points out in his book *For the Love of Language*, the ideal of linguistics is the reduction of language to its form, making of it an artifice of Sameness. Linguistics, circumventing nothing less than *lalangue*, strives not to attend to it in the least; linguistics is thus interested in language as an All and makes possible its object from the evasion of the *not-all*. What psychoanalysis reveals, on the other hand, from the formations of the unconscious, is that language is ultimately the non-identical to itself. The path traced, starting with Ferenczi, has let us approach that disparity of language with respect to itself. That disparity is what allows language to become fertile territory, so that on it desire may be channeled and the lapsus emerge. How can language be treated as if no one spoke it? That is to exclude completely the desiring dimension of speech.

The ground that makes up the Ferenczian opening to the traumatic dimension of language is made more complex when we find that in language dwells the impossible; not everything can be said. That not-everything of language is its place of kinship with the real. But the not-said of language is not complete negativity, the absence of signifiers to name the All, but positivity, because it empowers language: the latter exists because the not-said inscribes itself as positivity in it.

The difficulty arises when we attempt to produce a writing that allows us to preserve the presence of the not-said of language. Writing, if it is writing of All, must turn its back completely to the obstinacy of the not-said. Analytic experience allows us to infer that there is something of the language dimension that speaking beings will never own but will always be responsible for (which is a point of difference with Milner, 1978, p. 120).

Regarding this point, we raised with Levinas the following question: How can we have a language which is not negation of the other? At one level we said that it is impossible: language—and speaking—is always speaking of the Same. But, at another level, the fact that there is language implies that in it dwells, as potential, what is not said and this, as such, always occurs in the place of the imperceptible, of the non-symmetric, that is, of the impossible of communication.

With Benjamin, we suggested that the translator is a kind of *eromenos*. The difference in Greek between *erastés* and *eromenos* saves us from a more popular vision according to which lovers would be on equal terms: I love you and you love me; I love in you and you in me. If there is anything that veils the masquerade of falling in love, it is the disparity between the desiring bodies. The language between bodies that speak, namely, communication, tries, just like in love, to veil the imperceptible dissymmetry of the speaking entities (*parlentes*). Communication and love veil the difference as impossibility. The persistence of desire will always be the unavoidable remnant of immanent difference. Desire is Zeus's own thunderbolt which makes of the androgynous not a Two but a One, and a One whose summation, being an imaginary reversibility, does not reassemble—due to an internal impossibility—the previous Whole.

Does the real disturb language? We will probably be unable to answer this question without simultaneously adopting a stance of good faith. We have seen that it is possible to circumvent it, surround it, touch it, caress it, smell it, but nothing lets us know that it affects the real. New investigations can probably take up the aspects that have not yet been addressed but which might have been suggested by this study. Nevertheless, we see that the analyst, like the poet, tries to chart a course that is the writing of that which is impossible to write: writing about that which insists in clinical work as the real of language. Perhaps this is the point at which Lacan, producing from psychoanalysis, manages to overcome the ground that he started from. In the return to Ferenczi, made possible because of Lacan's return to Freud, we find in the *confusion of tongues* the footprint of that persistence.

CHAPTER FOURTEEN

Final considerations

> "Good-bye dear Karinthy, I leave you; but if I must be frank,
> I do not think that this farewell is final; something inside me tells
> me rather: I'll see you soon."
> "Science that lulls and science that awakens." A letter to
> Frigyes Karinthy, (Ferenczi, 1924b)

The contributions of the present study have touched upon three essential issues. The first has to do with the re-reading of Ferenczi's work related to the confusion of tongues. This journey has allowed us to see how Ferenczi's legacy for all analysts, not only referred to in his last writings but also in his written and clinical work, carried out throughout his life, makes us realise that the problem of trauma for psychoanalysis has nothing to do with technique; structurally, there is something banished from language itself. For this reason, all claims to offer therapeutic techniques as being the most appropriate, inasmuch as they allow a total inscription of all vestiges of the traumatic, implies compulsively returning to the dream of sense, to not awakening to the confusion of tongues. The unyielding aspect of trauma is not a flaw of the word, a poorness of signifiers, but that structural aspect that produces language itself.

This operation carried out on Ferenczi's oeuvre links it with Lacan's work, particularly in the formulation introduced in this study regarding "language trauma" or the "traumatic dimension of trauma". In this regard, it is possible to find in Ferenczi an anticipation of the issues that will find their place more clearly in Lacan's teaching (Gutiérrez-Peláez, 2015).

The second question addresses a key issue in psychoanalysis, nodal to the subject and therefore to clinical practice, which has to do with the real. Like all topics, especially in the case of the real, being outside the symbolic, one of the several possible (possible for an impossibility) means of access had to be used. In this case, the use of Ferenczian theory regarding trauma and the confusion of tongues was the perfect path that allowed us to approach and edge up to the issue of the real. In fact, circumscribing something of this kind is one of the legacies of this study.

With respect to the cure, psychoanalysis deals with nothing less than Being and the truth of the subject, that is, with the real as the singular substrate of the speaking subject, and this constitutes, therefore, the horizon of its practice. Regardless of the different instances, tools, and processes involved in the cure, what summons us to work is the subject's relationship with the real. The issue of the real—and its relation with trauma and language—is what we have attempted to present in this study.

It is possible to infer that the conclusions arising from this study are very important for clinical practice. At present, with the rapid advance of treatments that promise better results and greater efficiency, *therapeutics* works from the premise of the omnipotence of sense before the inscription of trauma. Only psychoanalysis—and this is a nodal point of Ferenczian traumatic theory—is alert to, and allows for a place in, the aspect of trauma that is evasive to the *semantic fence* of the word. The analyst who does not lose sight of this irrefutability of the traumatic to sense allows, on the one hand, not getting lost in the mirage that the symbolic masquerade entails, ignoring all hints of the real; and, on the other, permits that irreducibility to find its place in clinical work, thus acquiring a presence.

With respect to this clinical dimension, it is possible to perceive the radical difference between carrying out a clinical work of sense and a clinical work of the real. As Jorge Alemán (2000) suggests, either psychoanalysis is no more than a permanent commentary or it touches something of the real (touching it in a different way to laying a veil of sense over it). Ferenczi, for his part, goes as far as to think that the real is a problem of sense and a problem of technique: by changing the technique, a new place in sense can be introduced for the traumatic. But Ferenczi himself also realises that, despite his technical innovations, an evasive aspect of trauma prevails that does not manage to articulate itself symbolically.

Finally, we must refer to the juncture between contemporary philosophy and Ferenczi's thought, which allows his re-reading from the perspective of current philosophical debates, especially those related to language.

The journey we have undertaken has paved the way for new and further research that the length of this study has not permitted us to cover. However, although these issues remained unsettled in the present study, they have, at least, been raised. The re-reading of Ferenczi's oeuvre carried out in this investigation centred on his later works and mainly focused on the notion of "confusion of tongues", here dealt with as a concept. Nevertheless, another series of notions and concepts of similar rigour are present in the Hungarian psychoanalyst's work that could help to enlighten other aspects of contemporary psychoanalysis. Such is the case of his technical innovations (Gutiérrez-Peláez & Herrera, 2016)—his work regarding the end of analysis, his introduction and elaboration of the concept of introjection, how he treated the death drive in his later writings; even though they have been addressed, they have not yet been fully dealt with.

NOTES

Chapter Two

1. This corresponds to a posthumous paper entitled "Gedanken über das Trauma", published in the *Internationale Zeitschrift für Psychonalyse* (1934), which includes the chapters "Zur Psychologie der Erschütterung", "Zur Revision der Traumdeutung", and "Das Trauma in der Relaxationstechnik", published in English in "Notes and fragments" (1932c) as "On shock (*Erschütterung*)", "On the revision of the interpretation of dreams", and "Relaxation and education", respectively.

Chapter Six

1. It is worth mentioning, as Dupont (1995) clearly states in the introduction to *The Clinical Diary* (1932b), that Ferenczi never kissed his patients, but that this was a misunderstanding, a product of a comment of one of his analysands called Clara Thompson (another confusion of tongues).

Chapter Seven

1. We have preferred to use the term translation in a broad sense, going further than its linguistic meaning. As Derrida points out (1995a) when he refers to Schelling's conception of translation: "This justifies that, from the beginning of this lecture, I have frequently spoken of translation where I was really referring to transposition, transference, transport in a sense which is not strictly linguistic. Perhaps you might think I was taking liberties, speaking metaphorically of translation (taken for granted: strictly semiotic or linguistic) where the transposition to which I was referring precisely didn't have anything we could actually call linguistic. But it is precisely for Schelling, whose onto-theology I wanted to relate with what I've been saying, language is a live phenomenon; life or the living spirit speaks in the language and in the same way or nature is an author, the author of a book which must be translated with the competence of a philologist" (p. 75).
2. We cannot fail to mention the effect of italics or quotation marks on words, nor when they are written in capital letters, since it shifts the words to new semantic levels in such a way that the same word written in a different way is neither a homonym nor a synonym with respect to the other (see, in relation to the anasemic word: Derrida, 1997, pp. 74–75).

Chapter Eight

1. The end of analysis in Ferenczi, an issue that would require a separate study considering its complexity, is by no means closed with what has been proposed here. Following the thread of translation, according to Benjamin's journey, all endings would tend in any event to their infinitisation. But far from implying that in Ferenczi's case all ends are fictional, the end of analysis would be an effect of the analysis itself and not the decision of one of its parts: "The proper ending of an analysis is when neither the physician nor the patient puts an end to it, but when it dies of exhaustion" (Ferenczi, 1927, p. 85).

Chapter Nine

1. Translator's Note: In Spanish, the words "court" and "cut" are homophones.
2. We could establish an interesting relation between the kiss as translation (according to the way we addressed it from the *Küsstechnik*) and

this level of the death of God, appealing to Ferenczi's mother tongue, Hungarian, since "it's strange, but in Hungarian, those two words, killing and kiss, *ölés* and *ölelés*, are similar and have the same root ..." (Márai, 1999).

3. It is also worth remembering the strange case of Otto Rank, a "pure Nietzschean", who formed part of the intimate circle of first generation of analysts, also accepted as such by Deleuze, whose comments on Nietzsche's work are undoubtedly brilliant. Nevertheless, Rank's thinking ends up in the affirmation that birth trauma is the origin of all traumas. Thus, how can we reconcile this affirmation with Nietzsche's thought, so distant from a statement of this kind? The death of God is not only the death of the end, but also of the origin as foundation (on this topic see Zuleta, 2004, pp. 250–252).

Chapter Ten

1. Žižek (2003) distinguishes the imaginary, symbolic, and real dimension of the other: "In the first place, we have the imaginary other: other persons 'like me', the other human beings with whom I'm related through specular relationships of competition, mutual acknowledgment, etc. After that, we find the symbolic 'great Other': the 'substance' of our social existence, the impersonal set of rules that coordinate our coexistence. Finally, there is the Other qua real, the impossible Thing, the 'inhuman companion', the Other with whom the symmetric dialogue is impossible, mediated by the symbolic order" (p. 81). Nevertheless, it is important to observe that Žižek reads the issue of the other in Levinas as a metaphysic—different from the reading proposed here—where the face of the other functions like "the last FETISH" (p. 84), which helps to suture the great Other's castration. We, on the other hand, highlight that other as an opening to the real, as a way of exposing oneself to the impossible.

2. Letter to Georges Izambard, Charleville, 13 May 1871.

Chapter Eleven

1. We have proceeded in the same way with respect to the investigative method of the present study. Our method is not reading Ferenczi scientifically, but rather from a psychoanalytical point of view, which does not represent a deficit, but is consistent with a logic different from that of science. If we have maintained that Ferenczi can be placed within

the psychoanalytic movement, the reading of his work must be carried out with a method that is coherent with the logic that moved Freudian discovery and which is, ultimately, what determines what is or is not part of the psychoanalytical *movement*.

2. Let us remember the words introduced in *"Television"*: "I always tell the truth: not all of it, because we are unable to do so. Telling all the truth is materially impossible: there aren't enough words. Precisely due to this impossibility, truth always aspires to the real" (p. 83, my translation). In these words, the real is placed in the place of the impossible, not because it does not occur, but because it cannot be written.

Chapter Twelve

1. Fenichel (1939) uses the term to refer to Wilhem Reich's *Charakteranalyse* of 1933.

2. In the Spanish version of Ferenczi's work, what Freud had termed "etiological equation" in his first writings is translated as "etiological series". Later, in his twenty-second lecture from *Introductory Lectures on Psycho-Analysis* (1917), entitled "Some thoughts on development and regression—aetiology", Freud selects the more precise "complementary series", although not definitively (in the corrections he makes to *Three Essays on the Theory of Sexuality* (1905d) both concepts are kept). Nevertheless, we have preferred to use the term "etiological equation" instead of the one offered by the Spanish version of Ferenczi's work since, added to the difficulties with respect to the previously referred to translation, it lends itself to conceptual confusions. In addition, such a formulation was the one used at the time of the paper's presentation.

3. It is essential not to lose sight of the fact that Ferenczi takes up the role of "choice" in the result of a determined psychopathological profile. As Alemán (2003) correctly points out, "The only cases of non-reflexive choice are: Heidegger, Sartre, Lacan and Freud" (p. 24).

4. "Their silence runs the risk of duplicating the sarcastic warning the SS transmitted to the prisoners of the camps, which Levi transcribes at the beginning of *The Drowned and the Saved*: 'However the war may end, we have won the war against you; none of you will be left to bear witness, but even if someone were to survive, the world will not believe him. There will perhaps be suspicions, discussions, research by historians, but there will be no certainties, because we will destroy the evidence

together with you. And even if some proof should remain and some of you survive, people will say that the events you describe are too monstrous to be believed … We will be the ones to dictate the history of the Lagers" (quoted by Agamben, 1999, p. 157).

5. "Nevertheless, the same cameraman who had until then patiently lingered over naked bodies, over the terrible 'dolls' dismembered and stacked one on top of another, could not bear the sight of these half-living beings; he immediately began once again to show the cadavers. As Elias Canetti has noted, a heap of dead bodies is an ancient spectacle, one which has often satisfied the powerful. But the sight of *Muselmaner* is an absolutely new phenomenon, unbearable to human eyes" (Agamben, 1999, p. 51).

6. In her work "The constitution of subjectivity in Nietzsche" (2001, pp. 49–76), Mónica Cragnolini works on the notion of *Zwinchen* which, even if it does not appear formulated in this way in the German philosopher's work, allows us to understand the permanent tension of all subjectivity between the processes of identification—de-identification, subjectivation—de-subjectivation, consistent with the non-synthetisation of affirmation and negation in the construction of Nietzsche's philosophy.

REFERENCES

Abraham, K. (1907). The experiencing of sexual traumas as a form of sexual activity. In: *Selected Papers on Psychoanalysis* (pp. 47–63). London: Hogarth, 1927.

Abraham, N., & Torok, M. (1994). *The Shell and the Kernel: Renewals of Psychoanalysis (Vol. 1)*. Chicago: Chicago University Press.

Agamben, G. (1999). *Remnants of Auschwitz: The Witness and the Archive*. New York: Zone.

Agamben, G. (2005). ¿Qué es un dispositivo? Paper presented at the University of La Plata, La Plata, Argentina, October 2005.

Alemán, J. (1999). Introducción a la antifilosofía: La filosofía y su exterior. In: *Jacques Lacan y el debate posmoderno* (pp. 27–42). Buenos Aires: Filigrana, 2000.

Alemán, J. (2000). *Jacques Lacan y el debate posmoderno*. Buenos Aires: Filigrana.

Alemán, J. (2003). *Notas antifilosóficas*. Buenos Aires: Grama.

Alemán, J. (2006). *El porvenir del inconsciente*. Buenos Aires: Grama.

Anzieu, D. (1975). *L'Auto-Analyse de Freud et la Decourverte de la Psychanalyse (Vol. 1)*. Paris: Presses Universitaires de France.

Assmann, J. (1997). *Moses the Egyptian: The Memory of Egypt in Western Monotheism*. Cambridge, MA: Harvard University Press.

Auster, P. (1985). *The New York Trilogy*. London: Faber & Faber.

Barzilai, S. (1997). "History is not the Past": Lacan's critique of Ferenczi. *Psychoanalytic Review, 84*: 553–572.

Benet, J. (1990). *La construcción de la torre de Babel.* Madrid: Siruela.

Benjamin, W. (1918). Sobre el lenguaje en general y sobre el lenguaje de los humanos. In: *Iluminaciones IV. Para una crítica de la violencia y otros ensayos.* Madrid: Taurus, 1999.

Benjamin, W. (1936). The storyteller. In: D. J. Hale (Ed.), *The Novel: An Anthology of Criticism and Theory 1900–2000.* Malden, MA: Blackwell, 2006.

Berman, E. (1995). Confusion of tongues. *International Journal of Psycho-Analysis, 76*: 1045–1046.

Blum, H. P. (1994). The confusion of tongues and psychic trauma. *International Journal of Psycho-Analysis, 75*: 871–992.

Boorstin, D. J. (1994). *Los creadores.* Barcelona, España: Crítica.

Borges, J. L. (1944). Pierre Menard, autor del Quijote. In: *Ficciones (Obras completas, Vol. I.).* Madrid: Emecé, 1996.

Borges, J. L. (1949). El Aleph. In: *Ficciones (Obras completas, Vol. I.).* Madrid: Emecé, 1996.

Borges, J. L. (1964). El despertar. El otro, el mismo. *Obras completas.* España: Emecé.

Borges, J. L. (1984). Dos formas del insomnio. La cifra. *Obras completas.* España: Emecé.

Cragnolini, M. (2001). La constitución de la subjetividad en Nietzsche. Metáforas de la identidad. In: G. Meléndez (Ed.), *Nietzsche en perspectiva* (pp. 49–76). Bogotá: Pontificia Universidad Javeriana.

Cueto, E. (2006). Embajador del psicoanálisis. Entrevista a Jorge Alemán. *Imago Agenda, 105*: November.

Davoine, F., & Gaudillière, J. M. (2006). *Histoire et trauma: La folie des guerres.* Paris: Stock.

Deleuze, G. (1967). *Nietzsche y la filosofía.* Barcelona: Anagrama.

Derrida, J. (1985). "Des Tours de Babel" (trans. J. F. Graham In: J. F. Graham (Ed.), *Difference in Translation* (pp. 165–207). Ithaca, NY: Cornell University Press, 1985.

Derrida, J. (1995a). Teología de la traducción. In: *El lenguaje y las instituciones filosóficas.* Madrid: Paidós.

Derrida, J. (1995b). *Adieu to Emmanuel Levinas* (edited by W. Hamacher & D. E. Wellbery, translated by P.-A. Brault & M. Naas). Standford, CA: Stanford University Press, 1999.

Derrida, J. (1997). Yo—el psicoanálisis. In: *Cómo no hablar y otros textos.* Barcelona: Proyecto A.

Derrida, J. (1998). El suplemento de la cópula. In: *Márgenes de la filosofía.* Madrid: Cátedra.

Dupont, J. (1995). Introduction. In: J. Dupont (Ed.), M. Balint & N. Zarday Jackson (Trans.), *The Clinical Diary of Sándor Ferenczi* (pp. xi–xxvii). Cambridge, MA: Harvard University Press.

Eco, U. (1993). *La búsqueda de la lengua perfecta*. Barcelona: Crítica.

Eco, U. (1997). *¿En qué creen los que no creen?* Bogotá: Planeta.

Eribon, D. (1992). *Michel Foucault*. Barcelona: Anagrama.

Fenichel, O. (1939). Problems of Psychoanalytic Technique. *Psychoanalytic Quarterly, 8*: 438–470.

Ferenczi, S. (1899). Spiritizmus. *Gyógyászat, 30*: 477–479.

Ferenczi, S. (1901). A szerelem a tudomanyban [Love in science]. *Gyógyászat, 41*: 190–192.

Ferenczi, S. (1902). Homosexualities feminine. *Gyógyászat, 11*: 167–168.

Ferenczi, S. (1904). A hypnosis gyogyito ertekerol [The curative value of hypnosis]. *Gyógyászat, 52*: 820–822.

Ferenczi, S. (1906). Szexuális átmeneti fokozatokról [On sexual transitionary stages]. *Gyógyászat, 19*: 310–314.

Ferenczi, S. (1908). Psychoanalysis and education. In: M. Balint (Ed.), *Final Contributions to the Problems and Methods of Psycho-Analysis* (pp. 280–290). London: Hogarth, 1955.

Ferenczi, S. (1909). Introjection and transference. In: E. Jones (Trans.), *First Contributions to Psycho-Analysis* (pp. 35–93). London: Hogarth, 1952.

Ferenczi, S. (1912). The symbolic representation of the pleasures and reality principles in the Oedipus myth. In: E. Jones (Trans.), *First Contributions to Psycho-Analysis* (pp. 253–281). London: Hogarth, 1952.

Ferenczi, S. (1913a). Stages in the development of the sense of reality. In: E. Jones (Trans.), *First Contributions to Psycho-Analysis* (pp. 213–239). London: Hogarth, 1952.

Ferenczi, S. (1913b). A little chanticleer. In: E. Jones (Trans.), *First Contributions to Psycho-Analysis* (pp. 240–252). London: Hogarth, 1952.

Ferenczi, S. (1916). Two types of war neuroses. In: J. Rickman (Ed.), *Further Contributions to the Theory and Technique of Psychoanalysis* (pp. 124–141). London: Karnac, 2002.

Ferenczi, S. (1917). The psychic consequences of a "castration" in childhood. In: J. Rickman (Ed.), *Further Contributions to the Theory and Technique of Psychoanalysis* (pp. 244–248). London: Karnac, 2002.

Ferenczi, S. (1918). Psychoanalysis of war neuroses. In: S. Ferenczi, K. Abraham, E. Simmel & E. Jones, *Psycho-analysis and the War Neuroses*. Vienna: International Psychoanalytic Press, 1921.

Ferenczi, S. (1919). An attempted explanation of some hysterical stigmata. In: J. Rickman (Ed.), *Further Contributions to the Theory and Technique of Psychoanalysis* (pp. 110–117). London: Karnac, 2002.

Ferenczi, S. (1923). Der traum vom "gelehrten Säugling." *Internationale Zeitschrift fürärztliche Psychoanalyse, IX*: 70.

Ferenczi, S. (1924a). *Thalassa: A Theory of Genitality.* New York, NY: Norton, 1968.

Ferenczi, S. (1924b). "Science that lulls and science that awakens." (A letter to Frigyes Karinthy.) *Nyugat, 17*: 72–73.

Ferenczi, S. (1927). The problem of the termination of the analysis. In: M. Balint (Ed.), *Final Contributions to the Problems and Methods of Psychoanalysis* (pp. 77–86). London: Hogarth, 1955.

Ferenczi, S. (1928). The adaptation of the family to the child. In: M. Balint (Ed.), *Final Contributions to the Problems and Methods of Psycho-analysis* (pp. 61–76). London: Hogarth, 1955.

Ferenczi, S. (1929). The unwelcome child and his death instinct. In: M. Balint (Ed.), *Final Contributions to the Problems and Methods of Psycho-analysis* (pp. 108–125). London: Hogarth, 1955.

Ferenczi, S. (1931). Child-analysis in the analysis of adults. In: M. Balint (Ed.), *Final Contributions to the Problems and Methods of Psycho-analysis* (pp. 126–142). London: Hogarth, 1955.

Ferenczi, S. (1932a). Confusion of tongues between adults and the child. *The International Journal of Psycho-Analysis, 33*: 225–230, 1949.

Ferenczi, S. (1932b). *The Clinical Diary of Sándor Ferenczi* (edited by J. Dupont, translated by M. Balint & N. Zarday Jackson). Cambridge, MA: Harvard University Press, 1995.

Ferenczi, S. (1932c). Notes and fragments. In: M. Balint (Ed.), *Final Contributions to the Problems and Methods of Psycho-analysis* (pp. 216–279). London: Hogarth, 1955.

Ferenczi, S. (1934). Gedanken über das Trauma [Reflections on trauma]. *Internationale Zeitschrift für Psychonalyse, 20*: 5–12.

Ferenczi, S. (1955). *Final Contributions to the Problems and Methods of Psycho-analysis* (edited by M. Balint, translated by E. Mosbacher et al.). London: Hogarth.

Ferenczi, S., & Rank, O. (1924). *The Development of Psycho-Analysis* (translated by C. Newton). New York: Nervous and Mental Disease Publishing Company, 1925. Retrieved from: http://psycnet.apa.org/books/10664.

Forster, R. (2006). El otro, lo otro, los otros en Benjamin, Levinas y Blanchot. PhD seminar presented at the Facultad de Filosofía y Letras, Universidad de Buenos Aires, in collaboration with the Asociación Psicoanalítica Argentina, Buenos Aires, Argentina.

Foucault, M. (1963). *Death and the Labyrinth: The World of Raymond Roussel* (translated by C. Ruas. London: Continuum, 2004.

Foucault, M. (1984). *¿Qué es un autor?* México: Ediciones populares.

Freud, S. (1896b). Further remarks on the neuro-psychoses of defence. *S. E.*, *3*: 159–188. London: Hogarth.

Freud, S. (1897e). Letter 69, (Extracts from the Fliess papers). *S. E.*, *1*: 259–260. London: Hogarth.

Freud, S. (1905d). *Three Essays on the Theory of Sexuality*. *S. E.*, *7*: 123–246. London: Hogarth Press.

Freud, S. (1912–1913). Totem and taboo. *S. E.*, *13*: 1–163. London: Hogarth.

Freud, S. (1914d). On the history of the psycho-analytic movement. *S. E.*, *14*: 7–66.

Freud, S. (1915c). Instincts and their vicissitudes. *S. E.*, *14*: 109–140. London: Hogarth.

Freud, S. (1916d). Some character-types met with in psycho-analytic work. *S. E.*, *14*: 309–333. London: Hogarth.

Freud, S. (1917). *Introductory Lectures on Psycho-Analysis, Part III. S. E.*, *16*. London: Hogarth.

Freud, S. (1918b). History of an infantile neurosis. *S. E.*, *17*: 1–124. London: Hogarth.

Freud, S. (1919d). Introduction to *Psycho-Analysis and the War Neuroses. S. E.*, *17*: 205–216. London: Hogarth.

Freud, S. (1919h). The "uncanny". *S. E.*, *17*: 217–252. London: Hogarth.

Freud, S. (1920g). *Beyond the Pleasure Principle. S. E.*, *18*: 1–64. London: Hogarth.

Freud, S. (1921). *Group Psychology and the Analysis of the Ego. S. E.*, *18*: 65–144. London: Hogarth.

Freud, S. (1923b). *The Ego and the Id. S. E.*, *19*: 1–66. London: Hogarth.

Freud, S. (1925d). An autobiographical study. *S. E.*, *20*: 1–74. London: Hogarth.

Freud, S. (1926d). *Inhibitions, Symptoms and Anxiety. S. E.*, *20*: 77–178. London: Hogarth.

Freud, S. (1930a). *Civilization and its Discontents. S. E.*, *21*: 59–198. London: Hogarth.

Freud, S. (1933b). *Why War? S. E.*, *22*: 197–218. London: Hogarth.

Freud, S. (1939a). *Moses and Monotheism S. E.*, *23*: 3–140. London: Hogarth.

Freud, S. (1940). *An Outline of Psycho-Analysis. S. E.*, *23*: 139–208. London: Hogarth.

Fromm, E. (1959). *Sigmund Freud's Mission*. New York: Harper & Row.

Fulcanelli (1922). *Le Mystère des Cathèdrales* (trans. M. Sworder). Las Vegas, NV: Brotherhood of Life, 2000.

Granoff, W. (1984). Freud escritor: ¿traducir o estandarizar? In: *Lacan, Ferenczi y Freud*. Buenos Aires: L'école lacanienne de psychanalyse, 2004.

Granoff, W. (1997). Palabras sobre Jacques Lacan. El hilo ruso. In: *Lacan, Ferenczi y Freud*. Buenos Aires: L'école lacanienne de psychanalyse.

Graves, R. (1985). *Los mitos griegos* (Vols. I & II). Madrid: Alianza.

Guillot, D. E. (2006). Introducción. In: E. Levinas, *Totalidad e infinito*. Salamanca: Sígueme.

Gutiérrez-Peláez, M. (2006). Splitting como concepto en la obra de Sándor Ferenczi. Master's degree thesis, Universidad de Buenos Aires, Buenos Aires, Argentina.

Gutiérrez-Peláez, M. (2007). Sobre la traducción y la confusión de lenguas. *Revista Universitaria de Psicoanálisis, 7*: 51–69.

Gutiérrez-Peláez, M. (2008a). Las neurosis de guerra en la historia del movimiento psicoanalítico. *Revista Universitaria de Psicoanálisis, 8*: 203–216.

Gutiérrez-Peláez, M. (2008b). ¿Qué un otro *otro? Ideas y Valores: Revista Colombiana de Filosofía, 136*: 105–115.

Gutiérrez-Peláez, M. (2008c). La noción ferencziana de "Orpha". *Revista Psicoanálisis, XXX*: 285–290.

Gutiérrez-Peláez, M. (2009). Trauma theory in the 1931 and 1932 writings of Sándor Ferenczi. *International Journal of Psychoanalysis, 9*: 1745–8315.

Gutiérrez-Peláez, M. (2010). Diferencias entre los conceptos de *splitting* en Ferenczi y Spaltung en Freud. *Revista Universitas Psychologica, 9*: 469–483.

Gutiérrez-Peláez, M. (2015), Ferenczi's anticipation of the traumatic dimension of language: A meeting with Lacan. *Contemporary Psychoanalysis, 51*: 137–154.

Gutiérrez-Peláez, M., & Herrera, E. (2017a). Ambiente, trauma e innovaciones técnicas: tres articulaciones entre Donald W. Winnicott y Sándor Ferenczi. *Revista Colombiana de Psiquiatría, 46*: 121–126.

Gutiérrez-Peláez, M. (2017b). Contributions of psychoanalysis for psychosocial interventions in armed conflict scenarios. Peace and Conflict: Journal of Peace Psychology. Advance online publication. http://dx.doi.org/10.1037/pac0000270.

Gutiérrez-Peláez, M. (2017c). Retos para las intervenciones psicológicas y psicosociales en Colombia en el marco de la implementación de los acuerdos de paz entre el gobierno y las FARC-EP. *Avances en Psicología Latinoamericana, 35*: 1–8.

Harris, A., & Aron, L. (1997). Ferenczi's semiotic theory: Previews of postmodernism. *Psychoanalytic Inquiry, 17*: 522–534.

Haynal, A. (1997). For a metapsychology of the psychoanalyst: Sándor Ferenczi's quest. *Psychoanalytic Inquiry, 17*: 437–458.

Heidegger, M. (1955). *¿Qué es eso de filosofía?* Buenos Aires: Sur.

Hidas, G. (1993). History of Hungarian psychoanalysis. Paper presented at the Fourth International Conference of the Sándor Ferenczi Society, Budapest, Hungary, July 1993.

Jacobson, J. G. (1994). Signal affects and our psychoanalytic confusion of tongues. *Journal of the American Psychoanalytic Association, 42*: 15–42.

Jones, E. (1953). *The Life and Work of Sigmund Freud*. New York, NY: Basic.

Juliet, C. (2006). *Encuentros con Samuel Beckett*. Madrid: Siruela.

Kafka, F. (1920). El buitre. In: *La edificación de la Muralla China*. Buenos Aires: Losada. 2005.

Krull, M. (1979). *Freud und sein Vater: Die Entstehung der Psychoanalyse und Freuds ungelöste Vaterbindung*. Munich: C. H. Beck.

Lacan, J. (1954). El yo en la teoría de Freud. In: *Los seminarios* (Vol. II). Buenos Aires: Paidós.

Lacan, J. (1957–1958). De una cuestión preliminar a todo tratamiento posible de la psicosis. In: *Escritos 2*. Buenos Aires: Siglo XXI, 1975.

Lacan, J. (1958). La dirección de la cura y los principios de su poder. In: *Escritos II*. Buenos Aires: Siglo XXI, 1975.

Lacan, J. (1959). El deseo y su interpretación. In: *Los seminarios* (Vol. VI). Buenos Aires: Paidós.

Lacan, J. (1960–1961). La transferencia. In: *Los seminarios* (Vol. VIII). Buenos Aires: Paidós.

Lacan, J. (1964). Los cuatro conceptos fundamentales del psicoanálisis. In: *Los seminarios* (Vol. XI). Buenos Aires: Paidós.

Lacan, J. (1970). *Radiofonía y televisión*. Madrid: Anagrama, 1977.

Lacan, J. (1975). Peut-étre à Vincennes. *Ornicar?* 1: 5.

Laplanche, J., & Pontalis, J. B. (1996). *Diccionario de psicoanálisis*. Buenos Aires: Paidós.

Laurent, E. (2002). El revés del trauma. *Virtualia. Revista digital de la Escuela de Orientación Lacaniana*, II: 6.

Levinas, E. (1951). Is ontology fundamental? *Philosophy Today*, 33: 121–129, 1989.

Levinas (1961). *Totality and Infinity* (translated by A. Lingis). The Hague: Martinus Nijhoff, 1979.

Levinas, E. (1974). *Otherwise than Being, or, Beyond Essence* (translated by A. Lingis). London: Kluwer Academy, 1991.

López, H. (1990). Conferencia sobre Sándor Ferenczi. Conference given at the Universidad de Buenos Aires, Buenos Aires, Argentina, September, 1990.

López, H. (1994). *Psicoanálisis, un discurso en movimiento. Derivas del descubrimiento freudiano*. Buenos Aires: Biblos.

López, H. (2004). *Lo fundamental de Heidegger en Lacan*. Buenos Aires: Letra Viva.

López, H. (2007). *Las adiciones. Sus fundamentos clínicos*. Buenos Aires: Lazos.

López, H. (2010). *Sándor Ferenczi está de vuelta* [Sándor Ferenczi is back on track], retrieved from: http://www.elsigma.com/columnas/sandor-ferenczi-esta-de-vuelta/12056.

Márai, S. (1999). *El último encuentro*. Madrid: Salamandra.

Masson, J. M. (1984). *The Assault on Truth: Freud's Suppression of the Seduction Theory*. New York, NY: Farrar, Strauss & Giroux.

Miller, J.-A. (1986). Despertar. In: *Matemas I*. Buenos Aires: Manantial.

Miller, J.-A. (1987). Las respuestas de lo real. In: *Aspectos del malestar en la cultura*. Buenos Aires: Manantial.

Milner, J.-C. (1978). *El amor por la lengua*. Mexico: Nueva imagen.

Milton, J. (1667). *Paradise Lost*. In: D. Bush (Ed.), *Milton: Poetical Works*. Oxford: OUP, 1966.

Modell, A. H. (1991). A confusion of tongues, or whose reality is it? *Psychoanalytic Quarterly, 60*: 227–244.

Nietzsche, F. (1880). *El caminante y su sombra*. Madrid: Alianza, 1980.

Nietzsche, F. (1882). *The Gay Science* (edited by B. Williams, translated by J. Nauckhoff). Cambridge: CUP, 2001.

Nietzsche, F. (1883–1885). *Así habló Zaratustra*. Madrid: Alianza, 2003.

Nietzsche, F. (2006). *El nihilismo: Escritos póstumos*. Barcelona: Península.

Ospina, W. (2007). Una carta a Fernando Vallejo. *Revista Cromos, 4654*: 68–69.

Palnier, J.-M., & de Towarnicki, F. (1981). Conversación con Heidegger. *Revista Palos de la crítica, 4½*. Retrieved from: http://www.bolivare.unam.mx/cursos/TextosCurso10-1/CONVERSACI%D3N%20CON%20 HEIDEGGER.pdf.

Parrot, A. (1961). La torre de babel. In: *Cuadernos de arqueología bíblica*. Barcelona: Garriga.

Phillips, A. (1994). *Kissing, Tickling, and Being Bored*. Cambridge, MA: Harvard University Press.

Platón, (1962). *El banquete*. Madrid: Aguilar.

Press, J. (2006). Constructing the truth: From "Confusion of tongues" to "Constructions in analysis". *International Journal of Psychoanalysis, 87*: 519–537.

Rachman, A. W. (1989). Confusion of tongues: The Ferenczian metaphor for childhood seduction and emotional trauma. *Journal of the American Academy of Psychoanalysis, 17*: 181–205.

Rachman, A. W. (1997a). *Sándor Ferenczi: The Psychotherapist of Tenderness and Passion*. New York: Jason Aronson.

Rachman, A. W. (1997b). The suppression and censorship of Ferenczi's "Confusion of tongues" paper. *Psychoanalytic Inquiry: 17*, 459–485.

Rimbaud, A. (1871). *Cartas del vidente*. Madrid: Hiperión, 1995.

Roudinesco, E., & Plon, M. (1998). *Diccionario de psicoanálisis*. Buenos Aires: Paidós.

Sabourin, P. (1984). Prefacio. Visir secreto y cabeza de turco. In: S. Ferenczi, *Diario clínico. Sin simpatía no hay curación*. Buenos Aires: Amorrortu, 1932.

Saint Francis of Assisi (1390). *Little Flowers.* New York, NY: Cosimo, 2007.

Schur, M. (1972). *Freud: Living and Dying.* New York, NY: International Universities Press.

Sgalambro, M. (1996). El bien no puede fundarse en un Dios homicida. In: U. Eco & C. M. Martín, *¿En qué creen los que no creen?* (pp. 113–116). Bogotá: Planeta, 1998.

Silesius, J. A. (1675). *Peregrino Querubínico.* Recovered from: http://www.gnosisonline.org/wp-content/uploads/2010/06/Peregrino-Querubinico.pdf.

Stanton, M. (1997). *Sándor Ferenczi: Reconsiderando la técnica activa.* Santiago: Bio-Psique.

Sulloway, F. (1979). *Freud: Biologist of the Mind.* New York, NY: Basic.

Sylwan, B. (1984). An untoward event: Ou la guerre du trauma de Breuer a Freud de Jones a Ferenczi. *Cahiers Confrontation, 2*: 101–115.

Wallerstein, R. S. (1995). *The Talking Cures: The Psychoanalyses and the Psychotherapies.* New Haven, CT: Yale University Press.

Willson, P. (2004). *La constelación del sur: traductores y traducciones en la literatura argentina del siglo XX.* Buenos Aires: Siglo XXI.

Winnicott, C. (1989). D. W. W.: A reflection. In: C. Winnicott, R. Shepherd & M. Davies (Eds.), *Psycho-Analytic Explorations.* Cambridge, MA: Harvard University Press.

Winnicott, D. W. (1954). Aspectos metapsicológicos y clínicos de la regresión dentro del marco psicoanalítico. In: *Escritos de pediatría y psicoanálisis.* Barcelona: Laia.

Wittgenstein, L. (1922). *Tractatus Logio-Philosophicus* (translated by C. K. Ogden). London: Routledge, 2005.

Zaslow, S. L. (1988). Comments on "Confusion of tongues". *Contemporary Psychoanalysis, 24*: 211–224.

Žižek, S. (2003). Un alegato por la violencia ética. In: *Violencia en acto.* Buenos Aires: Paidós, 2004.

Žižek, S. (2004). El trauma: un señuelo engañoso. Conference given at the Asociación Psicoanalítica de Buenos Aires (APdeBA), Buenos Aires, Argentina, June 2004. Unpublished transcription.

Zuleta, E. (1980). Elogio a la dificultad. In: *Sobre la idealización de la vida personal y colectiva y otros ensayos.* Colombia: Procultura, 1985.

Zuleta, E. (2004). Controversia con Deleuze a propósito de "El antiedipo". In: *El pensamiento Psicoanalítico.* Medellín, Colombia: Hombre nuevo editores.

INDEX

175